Finding Peace In The Rain

By Sally Tippett Rains

Power Publishing
St. Louis, MO

Finding Peace In The Rain
By Sally Tippett Rains

ISBN 0-911921-72-9
Printed in the United States of America

All-Star Ideas
P.O. Box 270518
St. Louis, MO 63127
www.AllStarIdeas.com

Finding Peace In The Rain

Table Of Contents

Acknowledgements
Many sources were used in researching this book, and the books
and websites used are listed in the back of the book. I hope the
authors of the sources used are complimented that I used them
because I found them to be helpful, and I encourage the reader to
find out more about the sources used in the book.

Life is precious.
People are thinking about you and loving you right this minute, even though you may not realize it.

This book was written to give you hope and to let you know you are not alone in your fears, your worries, and your sorrows. The Lord is there and He wants to help you. If you look hard enough, there are also family members and friends who want to help you, but it takes some reaching down for you to be able to accept it.

You will be able to survive whatever it is you are going through. Things will get better. If today seems like a very bleak day, please hang on for tomorrow.

- Sally Tippett Rains

It is my hope that this book will bring peace and comfort to those who read it, but if you find yourself in a desperate situation and you cannot be calmed down, please call your local Life Crisis Center or suicide hotline (St. Louis: (314) 647-4357).

The national hotline is: 1-800-SUICIDE

Things can get better. Get better or get help.

Special Thanks

The following people contributed to this book either by giving their support, relating their experiences or writing an essay: Lisa Ingle, Angela Brunette, Theresia Metz, Nancy Newton, Sue Tozer, Tonee Guy. I thank you all very much.

To the many published writers who have inspired me in my time of need, especially Marianne Williamson, whose "Illuminated Prayers" was Nancy's last gift to me, as I found it among her prized possessions. If you see something they wrote which I used in this book and it helped you, please buy their books.

To Nancy and Anne. I am thankful that I got to know and love them in their lives and learn the many lessons which others have been able to learn from their deaths.

I will meet a million people in my lifetime, but these two will be etched in my heart forever and I will continue to dedicate my life to what I think God wants me to do and to carry on the lessons I have learned by being blessed enough to have been around them.

Thank you to Ken Christian of Power Publishing for his help and for publishing this book.

Dedication

Special thank you to Rob Rains, who is the most loyal friend and husband a person could ever ask for. His unconditional love, and the kindness he has shown me which at times was undeserved, is what (along with my tremendous faith in God and my family) has helped me move forward in this wonderful life I have been given. Rob never waivers in his faith in the Lord, in goodness, and in me.

I want to thank B.J. and Mike for being such thoughtful and caring sons.

A great bit of gratitude and love goes to the members of my family and friends who went through the journey with me.

I also wish to thank Rena. If you are ever going through a tough time, I wish for you a friend like Rena to go through it with you.

Romans 8:18 "I consider that the sufferings of this present time are not worth comparing with the glory about to be revealed to us."

Always move in a forward direction. Even though our daily problems may stop us along the way, never let your life's experiences push you backwards. You can do it, don't give up.

Chapter One
Finding God
In Everyday Life

You've got a lot on your mind. Whether you are working, taking out the trash, driving the kids (or grand-kids) to their baseball games, or running errands, you've got a lot to think about. If you are going through a tough time like an illness, a divorce or break-up, finan-cial problems or death of a loved one, it can almost seem unbearable.

How can you find peace through the storms of life? Sometimes the best way to put the worries of our everyday life out of our minds is through escapism. This is why reality shows, tabloid journalism, and 24-hour news programs are so popular. They allow us to escape our own lives and situtations and be in someone else's for just a while.

A good book can also serve as a way to "escape" your own situation for a while. Renting a movie is another way. Often, stepping out of our lives for a few minutes can rejuvenate us.

Another very good way to calm yourself down is to slip into God's world. You may not realize it on any given day, but He's standing right next to you and just waiting to be asked in for tea.

Make a Peaceful Place In Your Home

If you really want to find peace, a little planning will help. Make a special place in your house that is peaceful and and quiet. If you have a house full of children, you may need to do this before they wake up or after they go to bed.

Set peaceful things around you. What are some things that are special to you? Maybe a card given to you by someone special, a small gift, your Bible, and a candle. The candle is very important, because lighting a candle automatically brings warmth and peace.

The light of a candle will remind you of the light in your heart. No matter how hectic life gets, how tough it gets, there is always a light inside of you and it is important to never let that light die.

As you look at the light of a candle and watch it flicker, think about the times in your life when you were strong. That was when your flame was shining brightly. Sometimes, it is more weak; or the wind may cause it to flicker.

Never let the flame of hope in your heart go out. God carries us through the difficult times. No matter how difficult a situation may seem, his peace can help us through.

"But this precious treasure--this light and power that now shines within us--is held in a perishable container, that is, in our weak bodies. Everyone can see that the glorious power within must be from God and is not our own.

We are pressed on every side by troubles, but not crushed and broken. We are perplexed because we don't know why things happen as they do, but we don't give up and quit. We are hunted down but God never abandons us.

We get knocked down, but we get up again and keep going. These bodies of ours are constantly facing death just as Jesus did; so it is clear to all that it is only the living Christ within us who keeps us safe."

2 Corinthians 4:7-10

Let Your Light Shine

Remember this song...

This little light of mine--
I'm gonna let it shine.
This little light of mine--
I'm gonna let it shine.
This little light of mine--
I'm gonna let it shine,
Let it shine, let it shine, let it shine!

Each time you look at a candle, think of that flame as your own personal flame. Your flame is the hope in your heart and in your life. There is never, ever a day in your life when there is no hope. The situation may seem hopeless, but since we don't know what will come tomorrow, we can never really say there is no hope.

God Blesses Us Every Day
In Ways We Don't Even Realize.

He is there in the good and in the bad.

"That is why we never give up. Though our bodies are dying, our inner strength in the Lord is growing every day. These troubles and sufferings of ours are after all, quite small and won't last very long. Yet this short time of distress will result in God's richest blessing upon us forever and ever! So we do not look at what we see right now, the troubles all around us, but we look forward to the joys in heaven which we have not seen. The troubles will soon be over, but the joys to come will last forever."

2 Corinthians 4:16-18

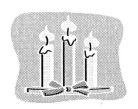

Find God in Your Successes...

Often when an athlete makes a great play, he or she will give credit to the Lord. Kurt Warner, a quarterback in the NFL, has faced criticism for this at times, but he never waivers. He gives all the credit for whatever he does to Jesus Christ.

His biggest success (besides his family) was winning the Superbowl in 1999. He used it as a platform to thank the Lord and to tell others about Him.

You don't have to be winning an award or the Superbowl to share your daily successes with God, just thank Him privately. Thank Him personally. Be grateful for every little blessing you have.

Don't just look for God when you are in trouble. He wants to share in your joys, your hopes, your dreams, and all of your many successes. Even when you are going through a tough time, you have things to thank God for.

Find God in Your Failures...

God doesn't want us to fail at anything. He doesn't want us to have bad days. When we have a good day, we thank and praise God. We should not give Him too much credit that He chose us personally to have that good day. This would lead us to the incorrect assumption that if something goes wrong, He deserves all the blame.

"God has a plan for our lives," is a statement we hear a lot. It is true, He has a plan for our lives, meaning our eternal lives. This little life we have on earth, this blip on the radar screen of eternity is not the only part of the plan. There are wonders awaiting that we can't know about right now.

Don't ever think that if things go wrong, God chose you to give bad luck to. He doesn't like one quarterback better than another, He doesn't make one person die and let one live because it fits His "plan" better.

If God Had a Plan for Me, Why Is Mine Not as Good as the Guy Next Door's?

This is where it gets tricky. There are different interpretations in the Bible, and people have different views on "why bad things happen to good people."

As a Christian who has suffered some unexplainable tragedies, I have reasoned out that God did not cause these things to happen, but He sure was with me at the times they did. He guided me all the way. His hands were on me and I could feel them. He never abandoned me, no matter how mad I got at him at times.

I remember being in a Bible Study during a very tough time and I read the verse, "The Lord takes pleasure in his people." (Psalm 149-4a) It made me so mad to read that. I thought, "Well if God takes pleasure in watching me, He sure is having a good laugh. I'm over here suffering and He is taking pleasure in it."

Sometimes when we are going through the valleys of life, our minds are not where they should be. Looking back on that, I can see I took it wrong. God does takes pleasure in us just as a parent delights in a child.

I love my children. From the time they were babies to the grown-up teenagers they have become, I love to be involved in their lives. I am delighted by them. When things go their way, I am thrilled for them and I am with them all the way. When things go bad for them, I am sad and I am also with them, giving them support and just loving them.

That is how God is. He is like a parent to us. Nothing gives Him more pleasure than to see us happy, just as we live for the smiles of our family members.

The Lord knows what is best for us. He knows when we are having difficulties and when we are having joys. As a loving parent, He likes it a lot better when things are going our way.

In times of trouble, it is God's loving arms that we can rest on. When you are feeling weak, scared, or upset, ask God to come into your life and wrap his arms around you.

"Now all praises to God for His wonderful kindness to us and His favor that He has poured out upon us, because we belong to His dearly loved Son. So overflowing is His kindness towards us that He took away all our sins through the blood of His Son, by whom we are saved and He has showered down upon us the richness of his grace--for how well He understands us and knows what is best for us at all times.

Ephesians 1:6-8

Dear Lord,

Things aren't going the way I wish they were. I am scared. Please comfort me and wrap me in your love. You have said you will be with us until the end, so right now I am asking you to be with me.

Let your peace enter my body and still the raging waters of my heart. As I call for you, I suddenly feel you here. You are right here in this room and I feel your gentle touch. Thank you for your love and for always being there when I call out for you.

May the peace that I am feeling right now stay in my heart as I seek to be a better person. I know I am better because you are here. AMEN

Be in God's Life And He Will Be in Yours

In good times, don't forget about the Lord. Rejoice for the things you have. Praise Him. Do the same thing when you are facing adversity. Rejoice for the things you have. Praise Him.

The Lord likes it a lot better when we are praising and thanking Him, even though we are facing bad times. It's easy to praise the Lord when things are going well. It takes some real faith to remember to thank God for the blessings He has given you when you're upset.

It is through trying times that you develop your relationship with the Lord. Just keep talking to Him. Keep the lines of communication open. Pray several times a day.

Go out into nature and see the wonders God has made for us. That is why hospitals often have beautiful gardens or walking paths around them. We find God in nature.

We also find Him in religious places, and that is why hospitals and funeral homes have chapels. Though God is right here, it is sometimes comforting for you to go to a place that makes you feel closer to Him. That is why making a little area in your house to pray is such a good idea. Go there and pray and you will be comforted.

I Corinthians 13:13- 14:1

"There are three things that remain...faith, hope and love...and the greatest of these is love. Let love be your greatest aim."

If you love the Lord He will know it and He will be your secret armor. He will be there for you, no matter what. It may seem like He is far away at times, but He isn't. He is right there beside you.

When you are worrying, look to the Lord, and rely on love to get you through. Love can help you through any situation. Nothing is so hopeless that love cannot come in and save the situation.

Even in death, love is there. When you lose someone you love, they become closer to you than they were when they were on earth. Their love encircles your body, your heart and your life. You feel them in everything.

If someone you love is far away, you can also feel their love. When families have struggles or friends have fights, if love is there, the situation can be worked out. Pray for peace and love in your heart, and the heart of everyone involved.

A gentle rain can be calming and peaceful; a storm can be scary--but a good relationship with God can make it possible to find peace in any type of rain.

Chapter Two

How Do I Live When My World Is Falling Apart?

If today is a scary day for you, take a deep breath and slowly exhale. If your world feels like it is falling apart and if you feel like your life has been changed, then maybe you feel like there is no way out. Well, there is, and it is through your faith and through prayer and through a personal relationship between you and the Lord.

Try to stay focussed on getting better and making it through this tough time. It might not be easy. In fact, chances are it is the toughest thing you have gone through. If you let Jesus guide your journey, you will make it safely through the storm and you will come out stronger and more graceful than you ever imagined yourself to be.

It may be hard to keep your mind on one thing, so this book is full of short, easy to read sections. If you don't feel like reading a story, turn to the Bible verses. If you don't feel like a Bible verse, just read a prayer.

Force yourself to smile when no one is looking, or when they are. Even a fake smile will bring those healthy endorphins that we miss out on when we are frowning, crying, and sad. They are important for our recovery, so make a conscious effort to smile several times a day, no matter how bad you are feeling.

On the days when you feel weak, tired and defeated, do something to make that day count. Just put one foot in front of the other and move. As long as you are moving forward in some small way, you are going in the right direction.

Even when things are tough for you, there is life going on around you and you should try to be in it. This is where it is good to learn to compartmentalize.

Compartmentalizing means to try to keep the bad parts of your life in one area and to be able to recognize that there is also some good. An example of this would be someone sitting at a loved one's side at the hospital. They may be worried, but it does the patient no good to see a worried face.

Take a walk outside, get a drink at the cafeteria, put the worries in one compartment and open up the next one...the one full of hope and encouragement. And while on the walk, notice the nature around you. That is part of the "goodness" going on in your world.

Dear Lord,

   Thank You for the flowers in my garden. Thank you for the puffy, white clouds that float through the vivid blue sky. The chirping of the birds and the blowing breeze are all reminders that you are here, and that you are in control. I am hurting right now. It is hard for me to find beauty in the world, but I will try. I give my troubles to you, o Lord, and I know you will see me through them. It is just so hard to make it through the day, but as I see the beautiful forces of nature you have put right before my eyes to remind me that you are there, I will trust you and lean on you. Please stay with me as I go through the journey of life.
AMEN

"I pray that, according to the riches of his glory, He may grant that you may be strengthened in your inner being with power through His spirit, and that Christ may dwell in your hearts through faith, as you are being rooted and grounded in love. I pray that you may have the power to comprehend, with all the saints what is the breadth and length and height and depth and to know the love of Christ that surpasses knowledge so that you may be filled with the fullness of God. "

Ephesians 3:16-21

Just Take Baby Steps

If all I can do is get out of my bed
Then at least that is one way I'm moving ahead.
I can only do the things each day that I'm able
Today I'll eat breakfast at the kitchen table.

Tomorrow I might feel better or best.
I'll aim for tomorrow to get up and get dressed.
The next day I'll walk to the mailbox at noon
The next night I'll go out to look at the moon.

For each little step that I'm taking each day
Is moving me forward and that's the best way.
I keep moving forward though sometimes it's tough
I'm doing ok, and ok's good enough.

Some day I'll be back to the me I once was.
My head won't be feeling like it's filled with fuzz.
My memory will come back and my tears may just stop.
Just keep taking baby steps and I'll be back on top.

OK Is Good Enough

When you are going through tough times, people ask, "How are you doing?" They are just trying to show their concern, but that's a hard question. If you say, "great" or "I'm fine, thank you," you may be missing a great opportunity to talk about your situation.

There are so many people who care for you and would like to help you through this, but they don't know what to say. Sometimes they say the wrong thing. They may act like everything is fine and try to talk to you about everything else in the world, except what your problem is, simply because they don't know what to say.

Then there are the people who say, "How ARE you?" and look at you with a sad face, trying to get you to talk to them about it. The problem is, this usually happens when you are coping well and you are in a strong position and don't want to get into a big conversation which might bring you down again.

Try to have empathy for those around you because they may not know how to behave towards you. Some people stop calling altogether because they don't want to "bother" you. If you want to talk to someone and they are not calling you, call them. Just as you are new to your situation, your friends and loved ones are new to you being in this situation, so you need to work together.

If someone asks you how you are and you say "I'm ok," and that's how you are feeling, then that's good enough. Don't feel like you have to put on like you are doing better than you are. Just getting by sometimes is enough.

Don't put pressure on yourself to be superhuman. If you don't feel up to talking on the phone, then don't do it. If you don't feel up to going out, then don't. You know how you are feeling, and you will get through it.

If someone is trying to help you, it is a good thing to let them. You may want to pass on going to dinner once, but if they ask twice, it just might do you some good to get out there.

Sometimes a person might give you a call and you don't feel like talking. Later that day you might be lonely and wish you had someone to talk to. Pick up the phone. We all need each other, and we need to help each other. We also need to let others know we need and appreciate them.

You may not believe it at this moment, but your feelings at this time will improve. Things may not be the same as they were, but you will be able to have a happy life some day. Just keep holding on until that day arrives. There may never be a "magic" day when it all changes for the good, but you will be surprised at how many beautiful moments you will experience if you will just let yourself enjoy them when they come.

Dear Lord,

Thank you for the blessings I've been given. Today I can't think of any of them because I am mad and I am sad. I feel like I will never be normal again. I will never be my old self again.

I am hurting, Lord. I'm hurting. Tears come easily today. I'm afraid and nothing is right.

Please wrap your loving arms around me and give me comfort. I know you are with me and I thank you for being here when I need you most. I can feel the warmth of your love.

Thank you for being right here in this room with me. You are giving me strength and I am feeling a little better just knowing you are here with me. You lift my burdens from me and lighten my load.

My heart is feeling lighter and hope is coming back into my heart. Please stay in my life, especially during this troubled time. AMEN

Dear Heavenly Father,
Thank you for giving me that extra bit of strength today. I felt better in the morning and was able to get some work done. Thank you for caring friends and family members who show me they are thinking of me, and thank you for those who silently pray for me every day, though I do not know it. Help me to grow stronger every day. I feel your love with me as I struggle to get some "normalcy" into my life. Please help me get better. AMEN

Isaiah 25:6-10

On this mountain the Lord of hosts will make for all peoples a feast of rich food, a feast of well-aged wines, of rich food filled with marrow, of well-aged wines strained clear. And he will destroy on this mountain the shroud that is cast over all peoples, the sheet that is spread over all nations; he will swallow up death forever. Then the Lord God will wipe away the tears from all faces, and the disgrace of his people he will take away from all the earth for the Lord has spoken. It will be said on that day, Lo, this is our God; we have waited for him so that he might save us. This is the Lord for whom we have waited: let us be glad and rejoice in his salvation.

Live By Faith

l live by faith--that's the only way
I can make it through my life on a worrisome day.
There are days when nothing is looking right
And it doesn't get better with the darknesss of night.

On the days when it all just seems so tough
When you're tired and weak and you've had enough.
Those are the days that you really must
Put your faith in someone you know and trust.

The Lord is there for us every day
Even on the days when we've lost our way.
Don't give up, stay straight as a board
And never ever waiver on your faith in the Lord.

Today is the first day of the rest of your life....

It will get better.

Keep believing and trusting that it will get better, because it will.

Someone is thinking about you right this very minute. A smile is crossing their face and you don't even know it. Think of someone who makes you smile. Do you feel like smiling? Say a prayer for that person.

You Make Me Smile

It is a great time to sit and think for a while
About you because you make me smile.
I'm sitting and thinking so peacefully.
I wonder if you are thinking of me.

My mind can see your face so bright
I'm thinking of you and it feels so right.
Good thoughts take the world's cares away.
I'm thinking of you in my mind today.

Dear Lord,

Thank you for my special person. I like thinking about that person because it brings a smile to my mind. There were happy times in my life, and I know there will be happy, calm, peaceful times in my life again.

I will think of joyous times I have had and build on those. My mind will always have the pictures of those fun times. No one can take that away from me.

Thank you, Lord, for the wonderful life I have had and for the wonderful life I have ahead of me. I will keep my faith in you, O Lord, and I know the future will be ok. Thank you for being here with me. AMEN

Think of someone who makes you smile or laugh and call them up.

Chapter Three
Be Good to Yourself

One of the biggest gifts you can give to yourself, if you are going through a tough time, is to be good to yourself. What has happened in your life is something you never expected. Whether you are experiencing fear because a family member is very ill, stress from losing your job, the turmoil of going through a divorce, sadness of a death or any other traumatic problem, you are probably just beside yourself with stress and fear.

Often when we are going through a tough situation, we feel we must be strong for others around us. We don't want others to feel sad or frightened, so we tend to overcompensate by becoming super-human.

While tending to our own situations, we have to go about the business of everyday life, which can become stressful and almost unbearable. It all seems to pile up.

Remember that you need to take care of youself while trying to take care of others. You want to stay strong for the others. With all that is going on, it is a struggle to do it, but try to be good to yourself physically, mentally, and spiritually.

> **"Life may not be the party we hoped for, but as long as we are here we might as well dance."**
>
> Author unknown

How to Take Care of Yourself Mentally

Try to stay alert and on top of things. During times when things are abnormal it is sometimes difficult to even remember what day it is. You can become so self-absorbed in your problems that you lose touch with the world.

A glance at the newspaper or the news will keep you up to date on the world and you'll know whether it's Thursday or Friday.

Another way to stay mentally fit is to step outside your own situation and think about others. Is it someone's birthday? Is your child going on a field trip? If so, you may need to send a permission slip. There are other things that need to get done and you don't want to fall too far behind if at all possible.

Watching a baseball game or playing cards with someone can occupy your mind with something other than your own worries.

How to Take Care of Yourself Spiritually

Pray, read your Bible, or do whatever you need to to stay in touch with God. You will want to rely on your faith to help you through this.

If You Talk to God Often, You Will Know His Voice and You Will Hear Him

Listening to hymns or singing them can be very comforting during your times of strife. The familiarity of a beautiful hymn can create a calmness in your soul. Christian music of all types will help you stay in God's world as you go through this.

God is there for you. He is right there beside you going through it with you. He'll be there every step of the way if you let Him.

God does not cause bad things to happen to us. We don't know why we have suffering, but we know that God does have a plan for us. It is too early in His plan for us to know what it is. Everything will be revealed to us in time and if we remain steadfast in our faith, we will be rewarded in Heaven.

This little life we have here on earth is only a blip on the radar screen of our eternal life. The Lord will comfort you if you let Him.

How to Take Care of Yourself Physically

Be sure to eat right. Whatever your situation is, you are probably either not hungry or eating too much. That is usually how it goes. Sometimes when we are upset, we can't eat, and then other times, we can't stop. Both are bad. Try to find something that you like; that you will be able to eat. At the same time be aware that if you give in to the "comfort foods" over a long period of time, your next problem will be all the weight you will gain.

It is nearly impossible to maintain your normal eating schedule when you are going through a stressful situation, and a little bit of weight gain or loss may just be part of the territory. Don't be too hard on yourself, you are doing the best you can.

Now is the time to drink a lot of water, take your vitamins, and remember to get some fruits and vegetables into you, even if you have to be creative to do it. You will need your stamina. People are depending on you and you are depending on yourself.

Try to fit in some exercise, even if it is just short walks. Moving around and staying active will help your well-being.

Relax....Easy for Me to Say!

When we are going through trying times, it is often hard for us to relax. You may find your muscles are tense, your face looks strained, and you may even be having backaches, headaches or stomachaches.

Take A Hot Shower

A nice, hot shower can help you "wash away your troubles" for just a few minutes. Make a concentrated effort to push your shoulders down as the warm water flows from your head to your toes. You might notice your shoulders and neck are very tense, so you will need to make the effort to relax them.

A nice, relaxing bubble bath is also a short break out of the ordinary and it can do you wonders.

Take the Time Out to RELAX - Here's How

R ejuvenate --Find the things that calm and relax you. Is it a bubble bath? Candles? Reading your favorite book?

E njoy --Do something that you like to do. Maybe you enjoy taking walks, going to a movie, doing crossword puzzles.

L isten --Listen to those inner messages around you. Find some quiet time to reflect and de-stress.

A ct --Do the things you need to get done. You will be amazed at the load you will be taking off your mind when you start crossing off things you have on your "to do" list.

e**X** it --Exit from the worries of the day. Make sure you get enough sleep. Remember, even when you can't get to sleep, you can lay there and relax,

Chapter Four
Words of Inspiration

"Don't Be Afraid." I can still hear Pope John Paul II saying that on the eve of the millennium. His words were a blessing to me, even though I am not Catholic.

Did you notice if the sun was out today, or if the flowers were in bloom? Did you see a butterfly or hear the soft musical tones of the chimes as they dance in the winds on a lazy spring afternoon? Whether it is winter, or summer, spring or fall, God has put beauty all around us, and even on our most difficult day, we can find it if we will just look.

People always say, 'no matter how bad your day is going, there is always someone who has it worse.' Well, you don't want to hear that. Each day when you wake up, can be a day you want to get up to, or the day can be something to be feared leaving you wanting to stay safely cuddled up under your covers. Choose to get up. If you are afraid, sad, or just mad when you wake up, think of something that will calm your mind. I like to go to the back door and open it up and just look outside to see what is going on.

Many days when I wake my sons, who are now teenagers, I say, "Wake Up! This is the day that the Lord has made! What should we do with it?" And they usually say, "Rejoice and be glad!" Sometimes they say, "Go back to bed!" but they are teenagers. I started that when they were young and it really is a great way to start the day. It gets you thinking in a positive way.

I enjoy looking for cardinals so the possibility is there that I might see one. I might also see a new blossom on the rose bush, or if it's early enough, there is the lovely orange and blue sunrise that I figure God put there just to brighten my day.

If you picked up a book called, "Finding Peace In The Rain" then you must be at your wit's end. I've been there, and I'm sure I will be there again. It's the way of the world. The Bible says, "to every thing, there is a season…" There is a time to be born and a time to die the verse says. A more modern version of this was Hawkeye Pierce in the television show M.A.S.H. saying, "There are two rules in war: Rule number one, young men die; rule number two, you can't change rule number one."

Hearing that doesn't make you feel any better for being in the situation you are in right now. The only way you think at this moment that you will ever feel better is for yourself or your loved one to get well, come back, or for your situation to change. The other way is if it had never happened; if there hadn't been a death, divorce, loss of job. Whatever caused the pain you are feeling right now has happened, and rule number two: you can't change rule number one.

There was a movie in which the kid asks his father, "Dad, when did life get so tough?" The dad said, "I think it all started the day the Yankees traded Roger Maris." There's always a defining moment.

You don't have to be a permanent victim of the tragedy or adversity that hits you for the rest of your life. Even though the times seem unbelievably tough right now, they will get better. Your life will be better than it is right now. You can wallow in it and feel sorry for yourself, and for a while people may even sympathize with you, but after a while you need to pick yourself up.

If you have lost your job and are having financial problems, you must be worried and constantly dodging the phone as bill collectors are calling. If they only knew what you were going through, but they don't. They are just doing their job. They don't realize how upsetting they can be to you.

If you are worried about a family member who is sick or if you yourself are faced with a life-threatening illness or condition, you are probably consumed with worry every day. What will tomorrow hold for you?

Those grieving the loss of a loved one are also uncertain as to how they will live their life. How will they live their life without this special significant person?

Probably the hardest thing to do when adversity hits you is to keep going, because at times you feel like giving up. Every day is a process. You have to put one foot in front of the other and keep walking. In saying this, the author does not wish to minimize anyone's pain, but just give you encouragement to go on.

You have someone who really needs you. You may not realize it at this moment, but someone out there loves you and looks up to you. Your parents, your child, your spouse, your friend, the old lady at church you smile at each week, the little girl next door who says hi to you. There is someone you really matter to and probably there are many, many people you really, really matter to.

I'm Mad Because My Prayers Didn't Get Answered

Everyone feels this way at some time in their lives. I prayed so hard for my sister to get well. She had bi-polar disease and they were giving her shock treatments. After the first two, she had one more to go, and as I drove up to her house to pick her up for the third one, I repeated my prayer. "Please God, please let this work, so she can get back to the old Nancy and she won't be in such pain."

The rest is history about how I ended up letting myself in the front door. When I could not find her at first and then realized she had locked her beloved dogs in the backyard, my heart sank.

As I ran through the apartment looking for her, my heart was pounding in fear. Suddenly, I literally felt a peace all around me and I looked to the right and there she was.

I don't understand bi-polar disease and I'm sure I never will, but I do understand the peace of God, which was all around me; incredible peace. I even felt like I saw a white, netting type thing covering her body when I found her. I know in my heart it was God's veil of peace there to help me endure what otherwise would have been unbearable.

I was able to make it through that day, comforting my parents, explaining it all to my sons, helping my sisters. God gave me incredible strength; I had supersonic strength that day.

Looking back on it, I realized I have had this peaceful strength at other times during my life, when I needed help. It is that peace that helps us keep going when a loved one is sick or we are going through a traumatic situation such as divorce or even victim of a crime. Though we are terrified, we are still able to keep going.

What if You Are Mad at God?

A couple of weeks after my sister died I was mad. I was so mad at God. For a while it was something I could not even say out loud. What kind of decent person who calls herself a Christian is "mad" at God? I was also mad at myself for having such little faith.

When you lose someone you love, your emotions range the gamut from sad to mad to peaceful to guilt and back to mad. Elisabeth Kubler-Ross mentions these stages of grief in her book *On Death and Dying,* and while I did feel all of them, I found they didn't go in any particular order. Even though I felt this wide range of emotions, I had the hardest time in dealing with being mad at God.

I just kept thinking, I can't be mad at God...but I was just SO mad!

After trying to deal with this on my own, I decided to talk to my minister, Phil Niblack. It was hard and embarrassing for me to say the words to a minister: *I'm mad at God.* I was surprised to find out he wasn't surprised. He also didn't think it was such a terrible thing.

The Reverend Niblack pointed out to me that just like with our parents, we can get angry with our Heavenly Father. When we get mad at our parents, or when our children get mad at us, there may be some angry stomps or some yelling, but through understanding we always get back together. A child generally does not stay mad at his father for very long. The father, likewise, generally does not throw the child out or give up on him.

That's how it is with the Lord. If we are staying near to the Lord in prayer and thought, the Lord understands when we get angry, and He loves us anyway, just as our parents did when we got mad at them. As my minister said, "Even when you are mad at God, you are in a conversation with Him."

It is through prayer and faith in the Lord, even when I was angry, that I realized that at my most horrific moment, God was right there with me, laying His veil of peace over me.

I don't know why Nancy had to die that day, but I do know she loved the Lord very much and when I found her she was already in His arms---and so was I. And really if I thought about it, she was out of her pain. It's hard to see this all at once, but the Lord is always there for us. He never leaves us.

I Don't Have the Strength to Help Those Who Need My Help

When our friend Bill was sick with a brain tumor, his wife and daughters were with him 24 hours a day. They cared for him, they cheered him up, they did whatever it is that families do when they are rallying around a sick loved one.

Bill's mother-in-law began having back pain, and one day she had a terrible stomachache. His wife was just torn because she needed to give all her attention to Bill and suddenly her mother was demanding so much attention, and besides all that, she was the mother of two teenagers--a demanding job in itself.

Sometimes when we are going through a rough time, either when we are grieving the loss of a loved one, or when we are spending so much time caring for a sick loved one, we think we need to be strong and take care of everyone, but we can't. After a while it takes a toll.

Remember one thing during this time. You are not Superman or Superwoman. Let others help you.

If someone asks, "Is there anything I can do?" let them bring you a meal or mow your lawn or whatever would help you out. This helps the person who is doing the asking because they are looking on helplessly trying to see how to make your life a little easier.

The one thing you don't want to do is work so hard on one project that you lose touch with the others around you. If you are experiencing a long illness of a loved one or if you are grieving the death of a loved one, then share your feelings with your family, don't shut yourself off.

Sometimes people don't want to let their children see them crying so they will avoid contact with them, farming them out to this relative or this friend. Actually, if you share your feelings with your family and friends then each of you will know where you are in the process and it is healthier.

If your father is getting older and needs more of your attention, you certainly should help him, but not at the expense of the rest of your family. This can cause strain on a marriage and also on a family unit. Try to think of creative ways you can include the whole family in helping to take care of dad, or try to get some additional help to take the entire burden off of you.

If you put your whole effort into your father, and your husband feels neglected and your children are running wild because you aren't there to supervise them, you aren't doing anyone any good.

When you are in a situation that all you can do is pray about, then you are undoubtedly in pain yourself. You are probably fearful about the outcome. This is the time you should be taking care of yourself, drawing upon support from your family and friends and relying on the Lord to go through it with you.

Romans 8:31 "What then are we to say about these things? If God is for us, who is against us?"

No One Has It as Bad as I Do

If you think you have had it the worst of anyone, unless your name is Caroline Kennedy Schlossberg, you haven't. Can you even imagine what it must have been like for her? Her baby brother died (Jackie had a son, Patrick, who lived a few days and then died), several months later her father is shot, Uncle Teddy is nearly killed in a plane crash, Uncle Bobby (her godfather) is shot dead. After her mother re-marries Aristotle Onassis, her stepbrother is killed in a plane crash, her stepfather dies, and then throughout her life, her stepsister dies, her only brother John dies, and several cousins die, all of tragic circumstances. How could a person like that go on?

Caroline Kennedy Schlossberg is a person I admire from afar because of the courage and example she has shown. Her heart might have been breaking but she put one foot in front of the other and kept moving. On the day of John's death from the airplane crash, Schlossberg was photographed taking a bike ride with her husband. She had children to live for, a husband to live for, and the memory of the loved ones she had lost to carry on.

When you are going through a tough time, try to find something meaningful in your life if you can't get out of the funk you are in. Volunteering is a good way. By helping other people, it helps you feel better even for just a while. If you can't find a way to volunteer for an organization look around you. There are so many people hurting besides you.

Bake someone cookies, send a cheerful card, call someone up. When you help brighten someone else's day it lifts the cloud in your own heart.

I still experience days where I feel like staying in bed and crying, but those are the days I force myself to get up and I call someone who needs a friend. I send a card to someone going through a tough time.

We don't know why things happen, we just know we have to trust God to help us keep going. It is in those times of deepest despair that we feel God lifting us up. When you are scared, pray to the Lord to give you peace in your heart and if you do that, He will. It's a done deal. I know that because it has happened to me.

Try to Live in the Moment

I listened to a woman named Cheryl give a speech at my church one day. She was a breast cancer survivor. She said that every day she would plan out a time when she could be alone in a peaceful corner of her house and light some candles and just talk to God.

One of the things that kept her going was to live in the "here and now." Be thankful for what you have at that moment, not that week, that day or even that hour. Just live in that one peaceful moment you are creating for yourself by being alone in prayer.

This woman is quite an inspiration to me and her strength gave me hope. She had no idea what an inspiration she was to me. You can be that inspiration to someone some day.`

Living in the moment seems like a cliché, but if you are ever actually able to do it, you will find those moments to be the most glorious and precious. If, during this difficult time, you live each moment to the fullest and appreciate the things you DO have, you will look back on this period and it will be a very special memory.

How Can I Live in the Moment?

When my niece was in the advanced stages of her brain cancer, my sister rented an eight bedroom house in Florida and invited our whole family down. She invited teachers, friends, family, anyone who loved my niece. Even though the little girl could not walk and was growing weak when she talked, we had so much fun.

If someone told a joke and Annie laughed, the whole room lit up. We would focus on what she COULD do and rejoice in every little event. Not once did we dwell on the bad news that the doctors had only given her several weeks to live. We didn't talk about dying--we talked about LIVING. When you are forced to live day to day you can do it. Our lives would be so much more blessed if we could enjoy every moment and not think about the future.

Thinking about the future causes worry and fear. It makes you afraid and when you are afraid you are not able to enjoy the days you DO have. One way to enjoy every day is to give your worries to the Lord. That may sound hard to do, but God wants us to do that. He wants our burdens.

While you may not find "closure" to your problems, and they might not all go away, you can certainly find strength in yourself and in your relationship with the Lord, as well as your friends and family.

Don't give up on life, don't ever give up on life. There is always a chance for a miracle.

Life Is a Gift

Life is a wonderful gift that God has given you and whether or not you know it, there are people out there who are counting on you. You matter to so many people, but especially, you matter to God. Even if you don't know Him. Even if you don't go to church.

God knows you and He loves you and He never gives up on you. It may seem like He does at times, but believe me, He never does. It is when you think He isn't there that He is doing his greatest work within you.

Just Don't Give Up

Never give up on yourself or anyone else. Forever is an awfully long time. Sometimes it takes little baby steps to get going. Sometimes you just have to be proud of yourself for getting out of bed (tomorrow you can work on getting dressed). Take small steps, but keep moving in the right direction. Reach down into that distant place inside of yourself that was the you that you used to be---the you that you want to be. You can be that person again, but don't rush it. Just keep walking in faith and you will soon be in the sun again.

If you are living in fear at this particular moment and you can't see the light at the end of the tunnel--just remember, the only reason you can't see the light is that there is a curve in the road. Stay focused and you will pass that curve and you will soon see that light. Wouldn't it be terrible if you just pulled over and gave up right when you were about to round the curve?

The Only Reason You Can't See The Light At The End Of The Tunnel Is Because There Is A Curve In The Road

Some of the reasons a person might be feeling fearful are the many changes that the human process goes through. Even though it seems like your problem is huge right now, there are others who have gone through something similar. If you could find them, maybe talking together would help.

Some people find support groups especially helpful for that reason. Small Bible study groups are a good place to meet people and pray for each other. When you pray for others, you realize they are hurting, too. While groups are good for some people, others would prefer to talk one on one with a special friend or a counselor.

Whatever helps you the best is what you should do. Keeping something bottled up inside yourself because you think no one wants to hear your problems is just plain dumb. It will come back to haunt you if you don't give your stresses and worries the time they deserve. (Don't give them too much time and go overboard, but you should respect your feelings and know they are real and you are entitled to them.)

Stay Positive

The more positive you are, the better chance you will have of coming out of your situation on top. Always think of what good can happen. Try not to dwell on the negatives. Ok, so you are scared, that's why you are reading this book, but the more times you fill your mind with 'what if…' and 'this could happen' or even 'why did this have to happen to me?' the more you will push yourself down and not bring yourself up.

Visualize Goodness

When my niece had a brain tumor, I would visualize the brain with no tumor. I always tried to be cheerful and positive. The whole family did this and soon my niece, feeling the positive vibes, joined in this upbeat outlook and it helped a lot in her recovery. When she was first diagnosed, she was not given long to live. Well, this little kid would have nothing of that diagnosis and neither would her parents.

They went to work calling friends and establishing a prayer chain network, and a friend put up a website to report her progress. The family stayed positive and focused on only good things. They went to the zoo, the park, the shopping mall. She had a miraculous recovery and went on to live four more years. You always have to think maybe the next child or person who outlives their diagnosis will be able to take advantage of a cure that is found during that time!

Medical experts will tell you that staying positive is a lot better than moping and feeling depressed about a medical condition. Also, by staying positive, you can keep yourself at your best and have the energy needed to go on the internet to look up possible cures and treatments, or read up about the studies being done.

The same positive attitude came in handy when my husband lost his job. If I were to fall apart and cry and mope all the time, how will he get his gumption up to go out and look for a job? Also, if we are depressed about it, that goes on out into the family, and soon the whole family is all worked up.

When handling a death, it becomes more difficult to be positive because you are so sad and overwhelmed. I remember saying to my family members on the morning that my sister was to be laid out at the funeral home: "We can go in there and be all sad (because of course we WERE sad) or we can try to enjoy ourselves seeing these people who we haven't seen in a long time and may not be seeing for a while (and then be sad later on.)"

It sounds crazy to think you could enjoy being in a funeral home, but so many family members and friends came and then there were neighbors we hadn't seen for years. We took the time to focus on them and the opportunity our tragedy brought for us to get together with them. Looking back on it, we all enjoyed seeing our friends, and I think our positive attitude helped those who had come to help us mourn.

It was a little embarrassing when my childhood friend, Darlene, and I were laughing out loud in the funeral parlor. She always could make me laugh harder than anyone. I mentioned someone who had come in earlier, and she remembered a story about them. Our laughter may have seemed inappropriate, but for those brief moments it felt good to laugh.

This is not to say you should not be true to your feelings. You should always be true to your feelings.

One of the most touching things I have ever experienced was watching a 280 pound NFL football player sobbing his eyes out at the funeral home. This particular player, who is a very famous defensive lineman and might be embarrassed if I used his name, was friends with my little niece.

He stood in line to pay his respects to the family, and as he approached the casket and saw the lifeless body of a person he had enjoyed so much during her life, it was too much for him and he was overcome with emotion. He knew everyone in the room knew who he was, but that didn't matter.

What mattered was that he had loved someone and lost them and the sadness flooded through his body pouring out large tears which spilled down his face. This display of emotion touched the family, and the shared hugs and conversation helped all of them as they started their struggle to comprehend life as it would be.

You can be true to your feelings while trying to maintain a positive attitude. Of course you may be feeling scared or worried, but you can do things to distract your mind. Trying to move forward in a positive motion is the best way to assure yourself of living a good life with a healthy attitude.

Finding Peace Through God

The old Beatles song, Let It Be, has the line, "When I find myself in times of trouble, Mother Mary comes to me, speaking words of wisdom, let it be." Whether you pray the novena or have a special relationship with Jesus Christ, or maybe you are Jewish and don't talk to Jesus, but speak directly to God, there is a peace that can be found by surrendering yourself to what some call the 'higher power.' Many call Him God and find comfort through His son, Jesus Christ. The following are some things that have given me comfort. I hope that if you enjoy the authors I mention, you will buy their books so you can read more. I am certainly not an expert, I look to others for suggestions and then I form my own way of thinking, as you should.

Try to Find Peace
In Your Everyday Life

Unhappiness does nothing to help your life. To survive in this world you have to be braver than you ever thought you could be. I suspect you are doing that. By spending a few minutes a day trying to capture the peace that certainly does pass understanding, you are being braver than you thought you could ever be.

Be Braver Than You Ever Thought You Could Be.

The things that have happened to you are things you never dreamed would happen. "Why" is a silly word. Never waste your time by saying, "Why me?" And especially don't ever ask "What else can go wrong?" because when you think you have hit rock bottom, don't worry, there is more room to go down. It is only when you think positive thoughts and try to pull yourself out of that hole that you will soar with the angels.

"Why" is the most common question we ask when faced with a tough time in our life. I have to admit I have wondered 'why' things have happened to my family, but I always try to end up that train of thought with a positive. I will never know "why" certain things have happened, but I know that I have a choice in my reaction to those things.

We Must Learn To Accept That There May Never Be An Answer To That One Question That Nags At Us..."Why?" Once You Accept There Will Never Be An Answer, You Will Finally Begin To Find Peace.

Wisdom Of A Child

Most everyone has seen the poetry books by Oprah Winfrey's friend, Mattie Stepanak, the little boy who was in a wheel chair. His disease kept him in a wheel chair and caused him many surgeries and hospital trips.

His mother must have been so frightened about his health, but he had such a wonderful attitude. He didn't dwell on his suffering, he wrote poetry and spoke to people and tried to spread joy wherever he went. HE tried to cheer OTHER people up, and in turn it helped him. There is even a collection of all of his books: *Heartsongs* by Mattie J. Stepanak. He wrote beautiful poetry.

Oprah Winfrey asked Mattie Stepanak "Do you ever ask yourself 'why me?'" He answered: 'Why NOT me?'

No one can tell you how you should be feeling or thinking right now. You are the only one who knows how it feels. That can be a real tough decision for you and one that causes stress because people try to tell you how you should be feeling.

There are people who are going to try to tell you you need counseling or you need therapy, or you need to go to church or take medicine. They are trying to help you, but ultimately it is up to you, and you have to do what you think you need to do to get better.

As long as you are moving forward, you are doing the right thing. During tough times we often think we need to stay home, because what would other people think if we were out having fun when we are going through all of this? Do what makes you feel better.

You should not feel like you have to go every time someone calls you, but on the other hand, if you are feeling like all you want to do is sit on the couch and cry, maybe it would be good to plan something. Go someplace, even if it is just to walk around the mall or take a walk outside.

Being with people will help you heal. Don't hide yourself away. There are so many times we are on our own, that if someone wants to help you or be with you, maybe you should consider letting them.

The main thing is do what YOU want to do if it is moving you ahead. No one knows exactly what you are going through except for you. It would make it so much simpler if those around us knew exactly how we felt, but that's impossible, that's why we are all so unique.

But I'm Just So Scared

If your fear at this moment is living in this world after someone you care about passes away, the best tribute you can show them is to carry on. It is God's will and the way of the world that people will die, but we can never know the exact date until it happens. We just live every moment. Some day we will all die, but until then, don't you ever stop living.

It's just so hard for those of us who are left behind or who fear that we will be, to go on. That's why it is important for us to live productive lives to honor them. Your loved one, whether very ill or deceased, wouldn't want you to remain helpless and sad, he or she would want you to live your life and be happy.

If your fear is regarding a situation such as a failing relationship, it may be causing you to become so crippled with that fear that you have trouble living your life. You have to dig deep to find the strength to keep going. Sometimes the worst part is the time you are in 'limbo.'

If it is a failing marriage and you know in your heart there is no fixing it, perhaps the indecision is what is eating away at your heart. Once you make the decision to either leave or to go into counseling and try to make a go of it, you will find a peaceful feeling come over you if you are praying through the difficulties.

That same type of gripping fear is experienced when we have health problems or one of our loved ones has health problems and we don't know what the outcome will be. Often just the worry of 'what if it's this?' or 'what if the tests show that?' can make the person even more sick. Stress from worry can literally rip at your stomach and cause illness.

Where there is worry and there is fear, there is an emptiness that can be filled with hope if you open your heart to it.

May the Lord come into your heart and fill that void.

Robert Schuller has a book called *Tough Times Never Last, But Tough People Do*. It's an inspirational book and he talks about being positive throughout adversity.

This is not to say you have to mask your feelings. Of course there is a process you will have to work through if you are having problems. A person can't expect to divorce the husband of her children and the next day live a normal, happy life. After a death, you are certainly not expected to host a birthday party. Allow yourself a few bad moments here and there.

When people are going through a tough time, they sometimes say, "I have good days and bad days." Don't judge things by a 'good day' or a 'bad day.' That's a very long time. Live for the moment. You may have some bad moments, but if you let yourself, you are in for some great moments.

"I've Been So Upset Lately, Will I Ever Get Back To Normal?"

Finding Joy Again

True joy can come back into your life, and it will if you open your heart to that possibility. Even in your toughest times, there is joy all around you. If you are spending a lot of time in a hospital, maybe you can take time to walk outside and look at the flowers, or go to the lobby to see the Christmas Tree, or take a walk down to the chapel and be calmed by the candles. Look for ways to find joy. Once you begin looking for joy, it will begin to find you.

Some things that can give you joy:

Birds

Have you ever taken the time to notice the birds? They are so unique, each one of them. Busily flitting around, singing happily, their songs really are peaceful and grounding. If you don't have a lot of birds outside your window, get a bird feeder. Figure out what types of birds you would like to see. You can attract Cardinals, Finches, Hummingbirds, all sorts of beautiful birds if you look on the package to see what the bird food attracts.

Butterflies

Butterflies can have the same affect on you as birds. They are so peaceful to watch flitting from flower to flower on a warm summer day. Certain flowers will attract butterflies and there are actually bushes called "Butterfly Bushes" that you can plant if you want to see bright, colorful monarchs and others. Butterflies signify, "new life."

Get a caterpillar and put it in a screen cage (you can make one or buy one). Caterpillars love milk week. In a while it will spin into a cocoon and then later it will open up and a lovely butterfly will emerge, its wings cascading out in spectacular color. They show us there is hope in every situation.

Gardening

Plant yourself a garden. If you enjoy and are able to do the planting, you can plant seeds and water them to watch them develop. Watching a plant grow gives you the hope that God is still out there and the world will go on and it will get more beautiful each day. There are so many blooming plants you can buy that are already started. All you have to do is put them in the ground. For those who don't want to mess with the soil and the garden, you can buy hanging baskets.

Nature

Any type of nature can really brighten your spirits. The outdoors is always a place of wonder. If you are able to go on hikes at parks, that is a great way to get exercise and just feel the joy of looking around at all God has created. Animals can be a source of joy. The zoo is full of wonder and if you haven't been to your local zoo in a while, maybe that is a fun activity you should consider doing.

One of the most joyful things you can experience in life is a sunset or a sunrise. The gorgeous colors splashed against the sky are different every day. I have always enjoyed the skies. My father and grandfather both made me appreciate the skies, be it when there is sun in it or when it is filled with stars. Looking at the stars can give you a peaceful and awe inspiring experience.

You can pay $7.50 for a movie but some people never even realize the amazing shows God puts on for you right in your own viewing area for free.

Now Showing:
(twice a day)
Sunrise and Sunset.

If you instill the love and appreciation of the heavens in your children, you won't be so surprised when your big 17 year old son, who was angry at you ten minutes ago for not giving him some money, comes running in to you and says, "Mom! Come look! The sunset is so pretty!" That is joy right there.

Pets

Pets can be a source of comfort when you are fearful, worried, stressed or upset. Taking a dog for a walk can lift your spirits almost as much as having him jump up on the couch to sit beside you when you are feeling down. If a cat or dog takes the time to come comfort you, notice it and let the pet help you.

Animals have a tremendous power in knowing just how and when to comfort us. That's why losing a pet can be so devastating. Your pet is your best friend at times and the only 'person' who truly understands you. If you are grieving the loss of your only pet, consider getting another one. Sometimes people are so hurt by the loss of a pet they decide they will never get another one. Try to remember all the joy that pet brought and if it's right for you, you won't be replacing your friend, you will just be getting another one.

Music

The right music can bring joy to you. Sad songs, of course, will get you down, but a beautiful Strauss waltz will surely lift your spirits. Lively music like rag-time and marches can liven things up. Hymns can also give you peace and joy. Ballads sung by your favorite singers and peaceful songs all can bring you happiness and contentment while you are listening.

Familiar songs are always a comfort. Musicals offer relief from the daily stress. They usually have a happy ending and the songs are lively. Playing songs from musicals can often calm a person down and change their frame of mind.

Friends and Family

When you are feeling low, you often feel like you'd be a burden to your friends or family if you called them. (Why would they want to talk to ME, I'm such a downer?) Friendship and talking to someone can help. Sometimes not talking about your situations, but calling a friend to do something out of the ordinary can be just what you need.

Don't hide yourself away. Make the first step. Sometimes people don't know what to say to you when you are going through tough times. Don't hold this against them. Right this very moment someone may be praying for you or thinking about you and wishing they could find a way to help. Help yourself and help them. Give them a call. Family and friends are truly one of life's joys.

If you can't bring yourself to visiting with a friend, at least reach out and ask someone to pray for you. If you know someone is praying for you, it makes all the difference in the world. God wants us to reach out to each other. Don't feel like you are a burden when you ask for prayers, that's the way it is supposed to work.

Reading

Get out and go to the bookstore or the library. Borrow a book from a friend. Dig out something you have but have never gotten around to reading. Books will take you far away from your problems. You can read 'how to' books to help you or you can read exciting novels to take you to a different life than the one you are having right now. Reading can be a real source of joy.

Magazines or the Movies

These may not really qualify as a source of 'joy,' but sometimes a form of escape can be a great thing. I know of a woman who reads People Magazine and watches the A & E Biography program, as well as the E! Entertainment profile shows. She gets so involved in other people's lives (movie stars, sports stars, etc.) that she feels like it is a little escape. Soap Operas or various television shows can do the same thing. Just a little variance in the routine of your day after your routine has come crashing down around you can help you cope.

Renting a video can also brighten your spirits. A lively, funny movie will help you forget your troubles. Another fun thing to do is to rent old movies, old musicals, or classics, things you may be familiar with. These types of movies can have a calming effect on you, taking you back to another time, when you were younger and watched them for the first time.

Church, Bible Studies, or other Fellowship

Peace and comfort can be found through your religion. If you are not someone who goes to church, you might consider trying it. You also might consider watching one of the Christian programs on television. For those who don't choose to go out to get their dose of fellowship, *The Hour of Power* (Robert Schuller), Jan and Paul Crouch on TBN, Chuck and Jenni Borsellino on *At Home Live with Chuck and Jenni*, Joyce Meyer, Taffy and Creflow Dollar and many others do a great job of both entertaining us, filling us with hope and comfort, and giving us Christian principles to lean on.

I have enjoyed Chuck and Jenni as they are a married couple who have children and acknowledge they are not perfect, yet they try every day to live the Christian life. I also think Chuck would get along great with my husband. They seem like just regular folks. You can check your local listings for them, but you can gain a feeling of fellowship when watching them or other shows like theirs.

There are some who think there is no substitute for the real thing and would recommend going to church. Since we don't know your individual circumstances, it's not for this book to preach to you to go to church. However having said that, church can be a wonderful place to go and hear the word of the Lord. You can meet people, make friends, join small groups and find a place to fit in. Great joy can be found in finding groups of people who truly care about you, and you can feel a certain sisterhood or brotherhood because of your faith.

Art

Artwork can bring a sense of tranquility and joy to someone who enjoys it. A trip to an art museum can be something that might change your mood. Art books are also fun. When a child is sick, often art therapy can provide much needed release and a sense of fun.

Art can help you improve your mood. If it is a particularly dreary day or cold wintry day, a quick trip to an art museum can lift your spirits. Thomas Kinkeade is an artist who can really inspire your mood with his beautiful use of light. He has comforting books full of pictures, and there are calendars and day books with his artwork in it.

On a dreary day when you need a pick-me-up, go to a mall that has a picture store and just look at Thomas Kinkeade's artwork. Looking at his art and reading the beautiful words of inspiration and the Bible verses he often puts in his art, is very relaxing and calming.

Speaking of cold, dreary days and bad weather, it is often on a cloudy day that your thoughts and feelings can become melancholy. If you have lost someone, a gray day may bring back sad memories.

Also, if you have experienced pain from a broken bone or arthritis, sometimes the weather can trigger more pain. When you are worried about something, the gray days make you worry even more.

Try to realize these things can happen. Sometimes it feels good to listen to a sad song and cry, but sometimes you need to move on and have things planned that will not bring you down.

There is a time to cry and be sad, but there are many great moments you will miss if you give in to your 'dreary days' too often, so if you are feeling down, go look at a beautiful piece of art.

Dear Lord,

I'm feeling blue today. There really doesn't seem to be anything extra wrong, but I just have that sad feeling. Please come into me and give me hope. Give me peace and a new outlook so that I may tackle the events of the day that I need to with strength and grace. Thank you for always being with me in my time of need. I know in my heart I have so much to be thankful for, please bring that healthy, happy feeling back into my heart. AMEN

"The only thing we have to fear is fear itself."

Franklin D. Roosevelt

The weather can play so much of a part in our mood, and sometimes if you realize this it will help you cope with that day. While a beautiful spring day can lift our spirits, a dull, winter day can lower them. Many poets, like the one below, like to compare the seasons of the year to the seasons of our lives. If that is a comparison, it's a great comfort to know that spring follows winter.

Remember the old television show, *Julia* from the 1970's. Diahann Carroll played a nurse, Julia Baker. Julia was a single mom raising her son, Corey. One night they had a visitor. Corey's friend, Earl J. Waggedorn, was spending the night because his parents were out of town. He was afraid and couldn't sleep. Julia comforted the boy with this line:

"No matter how long the night may seem, morning always comes."

It's the same with life, no matter how long the winter seems, spring always comes. Poets and writers have long used the imagery of the seasons when dramatizing a situation.

Everyone is afraid of something at some time. You may be feeling afraid right now. There is a a poem that compares the lovely changing colors of the leaves in October to the woman afraid of growing old. To go on with that thought, once she faces her fear, she can become peaceful in it.

Winter, like old age, is not just some bitter cold place with barren leaves. If peace is there, then autumn allows the release of those vibrant leaves, one by one, and slowly the ground becomes just as lovely with white, sparkling snow. It's different, but it is wonderful just the same.

That's how your life can be. If you slowly accept change and try to find a peace about it, you can live a happy and productive life. It may not be the way you would have envisioned it, but you can find joy in that life just the same.

Finding Comfort

If you go to the department stores you will see that fearful, stressed out people provide a good business for many people and now are a target market group for big companies. There are all sorts of things out there, and actually, they can help. Spending a little bit of time to take care of yourself will go a long way in helping you be at your best so you can cope with whatever is troubling you. You don't have to feel like you have to be perfect, but taking care of yourself can help you avoid getting sick, and it can help you stay strong so you will be able to be there for your loved ones.

Candles

Candles provide a comfort and should not be underestimated. If you are ever fearful, having trouble calming down, worried, or apprehensive, light some candles and sit in a quiet room and reflect. Having candles burning gives you a certain calm and clears your mind of whatever else is going on in your house or in the world.

Praying Or Reading The Bible

If you have a prayer book, Bible, or other type of calming book (like this one), you can read it. Praying to God to give you peace works. The next time you are fearful, go to a quiet part of your house, light some candles and ask God to come into your heart and give you peace. He will do it. It is amazing how quickly God will come to you and help you with your burdens. If you are truly seeking calm, and believe God is with you, you will be amazed at how this works.

Some people like to set up a special area in their house and set out comforting things, pictures, trinkets, family articles. They keep special books in that area and use it as their calm place.

Aromatherapy

This is a relaxing trend that is becoming very popular. There are several ways to use aromatherapy, candles, sprays, and bubble baths are a few. Just the words "calming" on the front of a bubble bath bottle might put you in the mood that this will do the trick. A lot of this is in your mind and frame of reference, but there is nothing wrong with buying into the popular culture and taking advantage of the products on the market.

Many women will buy a fragrance called "Beautiful" or "Lovely" when they want to feel that way. There is nothing wrong with buying something that says it will calm you down or take away the stress.

A nice bubble bath with a special aromatherapy added to it can calm you down. Sometimes music or candles can add to your pleasure. You are aiming for anything that takes you to a safe and calm place. Remember the old commercial, "Calgon, take me away!" That's what you are trying to do, just clear your mind of your troubles and concentrate on being peaceful.

Sound Machines

So often when we are stressed out or worried, sleepless nights can occur. The worst thing about not being able to sleep all night is the next day you feel awful. A sound machine is another gimmick on the market that can actually help you gently fall asleep. There are all sorts of sounds you can choose from. You can fall asleep by the sound of a train and imagine you are taking a trip, far, far, from your troubles.

You could fall asleep by the side of an ocean and imagine you are laying out on the beach. If you just want to fall asleep and have no thoughts, you could play a babbling brook. The babbling brook is so constant it puts you right to sleep.

Relaxation tapes and cds

There are many relaxation tapes on the market. You can buy the nature types of tapes that maybe have the sounds of birds singing or whales in the distance. These can be very helpful and work the same way as the sound machines.

There are also special tapes where people are talking to you and calming you down. Andrew Weil has a very nice, relaxing tape. He talks a bit and then they play musical tones and notes that get you to that level where you are so relaxed you will gently fall asleep.

Relaxation tapes can be excellent when you have someone in the hospital and you are constantly going back and forth. You may have trouble relaxing (and you may not even realize it). Take a few minutes out of your day and try to relax yourself.

Take Care Of Yourself

Getting To Sleep

Some of the previously mentioned ideas would help to get you to sleep. It's very important to try to get to sleep because lack of sleep causes you more problems than you think you already have. For one thing, as mentioned, you feel rotten the next day. Chances are you have a family and you need to be at your best, but if you are tired, you may be overly crabby, and emotional.

Every moment you are asleep is a moment you are not awake worrying, so sleep is valuable in that respect. You simply must try to get some sleep, for yourself and for your family.

There are all sorts of teas on the market made with chamomile, which is supposed to calm and relax. The old fashioned remedy is warm milk. You warm up some milk, but don't get it too hot. You can put some vanilla and sugar in it to flavor it up, or some chocolate to make hot chocolate. Some people like to drink a glass of wine to relax them.

One way to get to sleep is to tense up all of your muscles in your body. Start with your toes, and slowly go all the way up to your head. When you are all tensed up, slowly release and feel this release of tension. Take a big deep breath. Breath in….hold it for three counts and then slowly exhale. Do this three times, you will be so relaxed, you may soon fall asleep.

Another thing to do when you are trying to get to

sleep is to talk to God. Just lay there and be thankful you have this time to talk. Rather than look on it as a bad thing that you can't get to sleep, be thankful and say some prayers. You will probably fall asleep in the middle of a sentence.

If you really get desperate for some sleep, try this. Think of your front door, imagine what is next to it and begin naming in your mind where everything is. Go all around the room and then into the next room, naming, "there's the yellow lamp with the white shade, and it is on the brown table with the ornately carved wooden legs. On the table is a book and my reading glasses..." This tends to get so boring it puts you to sleep.

Headache, Stomachache and Generally Feeling Rotten

When we are involved in a situation where we have no control, it can often cause us a lot of stress. The stress can come out in many different ways and one of them is sickness. Headaches, stomachaches and backaches are common problems that may arise from stress. Try to eat right and get enough sleep as well as cutting back on your activities and responsibilities. Be sure to have salads and fruits included in your diet.

Naps

Sometimes just taking a pain reliever and a little nap will help get you back on your feet again. If you have a headache you can use some of those relaxation techniques to help you get to sleep.

Eat Right

If you are experiencing stomach pains associated with stress and worry, often just eating right will help. Even if you can't eat what you are supposed to eat, make sure you eat something. Dieting is not something you want to do when you are going through a traumatic time. Give yourself a break in this area. The one thing you need to remember is you may gain weight if you eat the wrong things. You need to accept this, and try not to go overboard because then that will be your next problem (taking the weight off) and we are trying to eliminate our problems here, not add more.

Finding Peace In Troubled Times

As pointed out in the above paragraphs, there are many ways to deal with stress and worry. Even though you feel your life is falling apart in some areas, it is up to you to keep trying and keep feeding yourself with positive thoughts and ideas.

If you are a parent of young children or teens, you will want to try to find peace for yourself so that you are able to handle what comes your way on a daily basis. Unfortunately, the world doesn't stop because you are going through a tough time. People need you. Actually, this is fortunate. It is what often keeps us going, just knowing others need us and they need us to be at our best or the best we can be at the time.

Don't be anxious about tomorrow. God will take care of your tomorrow too. Live one day at a time.
Matthew 6:34

Chapter Five
Favorite Bible Verses

You don't have to be a great biblical scholar to appreciate a good Bible verse. Some people only know one verse, but that may be something they can hold on to in times of trouble. This is a collection of Bible verses which have special meaning for the people who hold them in their hearts.

This chapter idea came from an article in *People Magazine* where Naomi Judd talked about her favorite Bible verse. I wrote it down and learned it, and it has become very special to me over the years. I taught it to my husband and children, and we all use it often.

It doesn't matter how rich or famous a person gets to be. We all have trials and tribulations. The successful people who stay grounded are the ones to whom their faith is important.

Some people like to memorize Bible verses. This can actually help you with your concentration. Others have a hard time memorizing them, but it is good if you could get one Bible verse that is your favorite; the one you call on whenever you need help.

If you find a verse that has special meaning, repeat it over and over and when you need it most, it will pop into your head.

Isaiah 26:3

He will keep in perfect peace all those who trust Him, whose thoughts turn often to the Lord.

Naomi Judd used that verse in her long journey to recovery from Hepatitis.

Philippians 4:13

For I can do everything God asks me to with the help of Christ who gives me the strength and power.

Kay Yow, North Carolina Sports Hall of Fame, Women's Sports Hall of Fame (for college coaching). Yow writes that verse when she signs autographs.

Romans 8:31

If God is for us, then who can be against us?

Adam Timmerman, St. Louis Rams offensive lineman

James 4:8

Come near to God and he will come near to you. (NIV)

Debbie Cooke Sweet, Rockford, IL
I have found this particularly true since I began BSF 5years ago and they taught me the way to study the Bible daily. God has indeed changed my life through those studies!

John 3:17

For God did not send his Son into the world to condemn the world, but to save the world through Him.

Andy Van Slyke, former major league baseball player ("John 3:16 gets all the attention, but I think people should look at John 3:17 too.")

2 Timothy 1:17
For the Holy Spirit, God's gift does not want you to be afraid of people, but to be wise and strong, and to love them and enjoy being with them.
Tom Osborne, US Congressman from Nebraska and former Nebraska football coach

Romans 12:1-2
I appeal to you therefore, brothers and sisters, by the mercies of God, to present your bodies as a living sacrifice, holy and acceptable to God, which is your spiritual worship. Do not be conformed of this world, but be transformed by the renewing of your minds, so that you may discern what is the will of God---what is good and acceptable and perfect.
Rick Horton, former major league baseball player, Director- St. Louis Fellowship of Christian Athletes

Mark 11: 22-24
In reply Jesus said to the diciples, "If you only have faith in God--this is the absolute truth--you can say to this Mount of Olives, "Rise up and fall into the Mediterranean," and your command will be obeyed. All that's required is that you really believe and have no doubt! Listen to me! You can pray for anything, and if you believe, you have it; it's yours!
Tonee Guy; She watched her brother on life support after a car accident. He made a full recovery.

Other favorite verses:

Psalm 9:9-10
The Lord is a refuge for the oppressed, a stronghold in the times of trouble. Those who know your name will trust in you, for you, Lord, have never forsaken those who seek you.

Proverbs 3:5,6
If you want favor with both God and man, and a reputation for good judgment and common sense, then trust the Lord completely; don't ever trust yourself. In everything you do, put God first, and he will direct you and crown your efforts with success.

1 John:3
See how very much our Heavenly father loves us, for he alows us to be called his children--think of it--and we really are! But since most people don't know God, naturrally they understand that we are his children. Yes, dear friends, we are already God's children, right now, and we can't even imagine what is is going to be like later on.

Galatians 5:22
But when the holy Spirit controls our lives, He will produce this kind of fruit in us: love, joy, peace, patience, kindness, goodness, faithfulness, gentleness, and self-control.

My Favorite Bible Verses:

_____

_____

_____

_____

_____

_____

_____

_____

_____

_____

_____

_____

_____

Chapter Six

Favorite Motivational Quotes or Sayings

Motivational Quotes and Affirmations

Many people find that motivational quotations and daily affirmations are very helpful. If you want to find many quotations, there are books in the bookstores or libraries or you can go to your favorite search engine on your computer and use the keyword "motivational quotations."

It can be helpful to take your favorite quote or affirmation and hang it up around your house.

We get so many negative messages every day that it is good to give ourselves positive messages. Type up some positive messages and put them in places you will be sure to see them: the bathroom mirror, the bedroom, front of the kitchen cabinets.

"This day is yours, don't throw it away. To the world you might be one person, but to one person you just might be the world."

anonymous

"Sleep means nothing to me. I can't wait to see the sun rise. I can't wait to let the dogs out."
Richard Simmons (on the E True Hollywood Story)

Work like you don't need the money. Dance like no one is watching. And love like you've never been hurt.
Mark Twain

Remain calm. Be kind.
Colin Powell

We can do no great things, only small things with great love.
Mother Teresa

Never replay the bad memories...only the good.
Mike Rains

Being a Christian doesn't mean you are perfect, it just means you are forgiven.
Tim Wakefield, former major league pitcher

The time has come to turn to God and reassert our trust in Him for the healing of America...our country is in need of and ready for a spiritual renewal..."
Ronald Reagan 1982

It is a great consolation for me to remember that the Lord, to whom I had drawn near in humble and child-like faith, has suffered and died for me, and that He will look on me in love and compassion.
Wolfgang Amadeus Mozart

No matter what happens, keep on beginning and failing. Each time you fail, start all over again, and you will grow stronger until you find that you have accomplished a purpose---not the one you began with perhaps, but one you will be glad to remember.
Anne Sullivan

If we'd only stop trying to be happy we'd have a pretty good time.
Edith Wharton

You can't shake hands with a clenched fist.
Indira Gandhi

Always look on the positive side to any situation, and if you want to achieve success you have to be dedicated.
Bonnie Blair, Olympic speed skating champion

Being a Christian doesn't mean that you are not going to have some trials along the way. Faith is realizing there is going to be some bad that comes along with the good.
Gene Stallings, former NFL and college football coach

I *thank God for my handicaps, for, through them, I have found myself, my work, and my God.*
Helen Keller

If you love, you will suffer, and if you do not love, you do not know the meaning of a Christian life.
Agatha Christie 1977

Today happens to be the Lord's Day, so I will quote you something from my Bible: "See that ye love one another as I have loved you."
Ludwig van Beethoven

Within your heart, keep one still, secret spot where dreams may go.
Louise Driscoll

You may not know what the future holds, but you know who holds the future.
John Stuper, World Series winning pitcher, Yale Baseball Coach

We all have ability. The difference is how we use it.
Stevie Wonder

The state of your life is nothing more than a reflection of your state of mind.
Dr. Wayne W. Dyer

No pessimist ever discovered the secrets of the stars, or sailed to an uncharted land, or opened a new heaven to the human spirit.
Helen Keller

Learn to get in touch with the silence within yourself and know that everything in this life has a purpose.
Elisabeth Kubler-Ross

Everything you need you already have. You are complete right now, you are a whole, total person, not an apprentice person on the way to someplace else. Your completeness must be understood by you and experienced in your thoughts as your own personal reality.
Wayne Dyer

Chapter Seven
The Power of Prayer
Stories of Miracle Proportions

Sometimes it's nice to know you are not alone with your problems. These are real stories from real people. Many were kind enough to share them with me so I could share them with you. I chose not to give their full names or exact locations to preserve their privacy, but the words are theirs. Remember, miracles come in all shapes and sizes.

In Their Own Words

Pastor Survives An Emergency Room Visit and Serious Illness

Mark, who was a pastor in Memphis, was vacationing in San Diego with his family. He and his wife and three young children were enjoying some recreation and family time together. He was playing golf when he had terrible stomach pains and began vomiting.

They took him to the emergency room and within 24 hours his organs began shutting down. The doctors diagnosed it as pancreatitis. He went into a coma and the doctors gave him a "token 1% chance of surviving."

His family, which was spread in different states began getting on the phone talking about it and praying about it. His sister-in-law runs a prayer chain and is a member on at least one other prayer chain and they got the prayer warriors in action.

Though it seemed so dim, they never lost hope. Everyone prayed, and thanks to God's mercy and His plan for Mark's life; he was healed and home within three weeks. The doctors were amazed at his recovery. After having been given a "one in 100 chance for survival" he's doing fine now and has a great testimony.

Prayers and Good Medical Care Cure Brain Tumor

Christa was in kindergarten when she started to stumble and become clumsy. Her parents became alarmed and took her to the hospital where she was diagnosed with a brain tumor. She had operation after operations causing her to miss school. She was not expected to survive.

Her parents, being of incredible strength, continued to lean on God. She had the whole school community praying for her. Slowly but surely she recovered. It was not an easy process. Academically she never lost so much ground that she was unable to catch up eventually.

I was a teacher and she was in my 4th grade science class. Her survival and her parents' faith is a testament to what God does in our lives. This little girl really worked. She had an incredible will to survive, function, and have fun. She is now in 8th grade...cancer free. She is not without some residual effects of the illness, but her faith and her family's faith have been inspirational for everyone they have touched.

Single Mom And Son Thrive After Husband Deserts Them

My husband left me and my son. It should not have been a surprise because he was growing farther and farther away from us. He traveled a lot and wasn't home even when he was in town. He hardly ever did anything with our son, who was starving for his affection.

At first our son was devastated and felt it was his fault. He went through some real trials. It's just with tremendous strength that we have conquered such an insane situation. Through adversity our faith has grown. It has been a welcomed source of comfort for us both.

My son is an incredible young man. I learn from his knowledge in the Lord everyday. He has definitely triumphed in the face of adversity. No one should have to suffer through a divorce, but if they lean on the Lord, their needs will be met (emotionally and physically).

Not a day goes by where someone at school tells me what a great kid I have. His maturity in his faith is unreal. He is the epitome of "I can do all things through Christ who strengthens me."

She's In Heaven With God

This is a story of someone who did not recover from her illness here on earth, but has gone to Heaven to live with the Lord and will never suffer again. Nancy was struggling with severe mental illness. People who don't understand mental illness have no concept of how painful it is to deal with the chemical imbalances of the body, which come from such diseases as manic depression and bi-polar disease.

She knew she was sick and she even checked herself into a hospital. Unfortunately, after she was discharged, and was undergoing outpatient shock therapy, the illness got the best of her. It was a terrible shock to her family, especially to her parents who had loved her dearly for all 40 years of her life.

The day after his daughter had passed away, Nancy's father got down on her knees and prayed to God. "Lord," he said. "Please Bless Nancy."

And then as he tells it: "I never knew I could cry tears of joy! The Lord said, 'Don't worry about her, I've got her right here in my arms.'"

As he became surrounded with the incredible peace that only God can give us, he knew his little girl was in Heaven and he wept. As he said, they were tears of joy because while he would miss her terribly, he knew she was safe and at peace, and for a father that was the greatest gift he could have been given at that time.

Music Saves The Patient

We had a patient named Mrs. G. when I was a nurses' aide who doctors didn't think would survive the trip to the hospital, then the hospital didn't think she'd survive, then she wasn't expected to make it to us. We had her on all kinds of support. The nurse assigned just one experienced aide to her daily care. The family had a radio next to the bed with a sign that said to keep it on the country station. That aide did a no-no--she heard God say put it on the Christian station and she switched it.

Mrs. G got better and better, and just amazed us. Every barrier where you'd think she'd stop, she'd break through. When she started talking, it was totally scrambled, unlike anything you've heard. Finally she could sit up in a chair (tied in) for a short bit, but had a stiff leg and couldn't walk. I came in one morning and everyone said, "Did you hear about Mrs G?" In the night she had gotten up, walked the entire long hall, pushed through two sets of heavy steel doors, and they found her sleeping on a load of laundry--little lady, impossible. We felt her recovery was from listening to Christian music.

In The Palm Of His Hand

My daughter had been in the doctor's office for a pulled muscle in her back. She was in pain, and after months of ibuprofen, it wasn't getting better. One night, I had a dream that a hand was coming down and I placed my daughter in this hand. Her head dropped back and she was limp. I realized my daughter was dead in the dream. I knew the hand was God's hand because I felt so much love for my little girl. I told God that you love my daughter even more than I and she's yours. I then begged that she would live and that she could use her talents to glorify Him!

A few weeks later, after a biopsy of her spine, we were told she had a malignant tumor on her spine. She was immediately admitted into the hospital and began receiving chemo. After she finally dropped off to sleep that night, I lost control and began crying. My husband asked my sister to drive me home as he was afraid I was disturbing other patients.

That night I was awakened at 3:23 a.m. with an awesome dream! My bedroom was totally white, clouds appeared and swirled back to make a scroll. The hand came down again - only this time it motioned to me that it was there to heal not to take her home. Angels were rejoicing, as were people on the earth! It was so exciting, I jumped out of bed and described it in my journal!

I felt so strongly I had had a vision, in fact I'm certain of it, and I was so calm and knew my little girl would be all right. She had malignant cancer and got so sick. People would tell me I have to 'face facts' that she would die, but I didn't believe it. Even though she got to the place where she had to go in a wheel chair and had no strength, I never gave up. I knew God had spoken to me. I remember a certain day when the doctors told us she would probably die the next day. She did survive and is now a beautiful teenager.

A Survivor

Seven years ago I (person telling the story) was diagnosed with breast cancer. By the time they found it it had metastisized and the prognosis was not good. I think that often times when something like this happens to a person, something huge changes in them. Some people hold on to their disease and that is who they are. I decided early on that I wasn't going to become "oh, poor me." Besides, I dislike, intensely, not having control over myself! I became a survivor, not a victim.

"Miracle Girl" CelebratesBat Mitzvah

The temple was packed with family and friends, and Sue was filled with joy as she looked out at the sea of smiling faces. People had flown in from all over the country. Her palms felt moist and her heart raced as she began to give the Bat Mitzvah speech about how much her daughter, Shana meant to her.

"When you were born, we were not handed a baby," she said, her voice unquavering. "We were handed a picture of a little baby hooked up to machines with tubes. They were not certain you would live, it was a very scary time."

Shana, a pretty brunette 13 year old watched her mother, waiting to hear what was to come next.

"Once it was established you would live, the doctors told us you would never walk," continued Sue. "Well you walked and you ran, and you played tennis, and you danced. You were a miracle."

There were very few dry eyes in the temple as they listened to the mother tell her daughter how special she was to her family. They have two other daughters who they love just as much, but standing in front of the crowd on this most special of all days, Sue reflected on the fact that they might not have been there if not for their faith and prayers. They refused to believe the negative diagnosis and always kept a positive attitude.

The theme of Shana's Bat Mitzvah reading was the book of Isaiah. Isiah's main message was to trust God, and that is what they did. As a young woman, she wanted to impart that wisdom on to others.

God's Tender Flower and Little Angel

My mother is schizophrenic (person telling the story) and has manic depression. It's been that way for as long as I have known her. There were four of us: Mom, dad, my sister and me. Growing up, our main concern was with my sister, who is mentally retarded. My mother controls her schizophrenia and depression when she maintains her medication. Throughout my life it has been a constant battle for my family. Mental illness is very difficult to deal with and to understand, but can be helped with the medication. Many people don't understand mental illness because it is a silent disease in many cases. On the outside people appear 'normal' when they take their medication. A lot goes on behind the scenes that the general public, who does not have a family member who suffers from mental illness does not realize.

I've watched friends who have suffered from terrible losses and I feel God spared my family of many other hardships, and I thank the Lord for it. Some may look at my situation and think I have been given a lot of difficulties. I don't feel that way because of the way my father looked at life.

.	I will carry the burden of mental illness with me forever. It was easier when I had my father to talk to. Recently I have gotten a divorce, so my support system has even been reduced more.

My father told me on his death bed..."Sometimes God gives us things that we have no control over," he said. "Your mother and sister were His gifts to us." He called my mom his "tender flower" and my sister his "little angel." When my mother or sister call I cannot say no, I must go and lend a hand. I never see them as a burden. They are our, as my father said, "gifts from God"--and that is how I deal with the sometime heavy burden that comes along with loving a family member who needs you so much.

He Was With Her During Surgery

I had to have a major cancer surgery (person telling the story) and everyone around me was worried, but I wasn't. During this time in my life, which was full of worries about the diagnois, and physical pain, I seemed to grow closer to God.

The day I went into surgery I felt God was with me. I told the nurse, "God is here, He is with me." I knew he was in the operating room: in the surgeon, even in the equipment. I could feel his presence everywhere and I still feel him now. There are so many people praying for me and I feel at peace because He is with me.

Miracles Happen Every Day

There are stories of miracles happening every day. Many people have felt the hand of God touch their lives. Paula Abdul, the popular American Idol host who was an award winning singer and dancer, considers her life to be a miracle. She was injured during the time she was a Laker Girl and suffered from a very painful disease.

Despite living with pain every day, she never gave up. She showed up for life every day. According to interviews with Abdul, the first year she did the Idol show she was in so much pain she had to jam her back into corners just so she could feel something other than the intense pain she was feeling.

One day she found the proper medicine and her pain was gone. So often this can happen in our lives. We are having problems and it seems so hopeless. If she had given up and stayed in bed with the pain, she would never have had the exciting episode in her life that American Idol has created.

Every day that we get up and live our life, we are closer to a breakthrough. It took me 10 years before my first book was published. I got so many 'reject letters,' I joked that I could wallpaper my bathroom with them. That's when it hit me, I got a notebook and wrote "wallpaper samples" on the outside and started saving my rejection letters.

When I turned 40, I got my first book published and then I had eight books published in the next eight years. What if I had given up after a few rejections?

Chapter Eight
Keeping Prayer in Your Life

With each dawning comes a new situation we must face, some good, some bad. In order to stay in harmony with the world, it is good to have a prayer life. Staying close to God will only help you, and it is something that the Lord wants us to do. Each day He wants us to rejoice and give thanks and praise for the good things that happen to us, and He also wants us to come to Him with the things that trouble us. By giving your troubles to the Lord, you can literally take a load off of your own shoulders.

Many people are afraid of prayer. They would shudder at the thought of praying out loud in a group prayer. Some still pray the childhood prayers they learned for lack of "knowing" how to pray. When we were children, many of our parents taught us the prayer, "Now I lay me down to sleep."

When you think about it, that prayer can be a very scary prayer to children because it talks about dying.

Our Childhood Prayer:
"Now I lay me down to sleep, I pray the Lord my soul to keep, If I should die before I wake, I pray the Lord my soul to take."

If you actually look at the words of that prayer, you can see why some people change the words a bit. The concept is good though because we are all praying for the Lord to bless us and keep us. We are hoping He doesn't take us too soon, but that's basically what the prayer is for.

As an adult we can pray the same thing. An easy way to pray is to start by thanking God for everything you have. Then after you have thanked Him, praise Him. Finally, ask the Lord to bless you and to bless those you are concerned with, and ask specifically for what you want.

Don't ever be afraid that what you are praying for is not important enough to be in a prayer. If it is important to you, it is important to God.

The Lord Taught Us...

In the Bible it says to pray the way the Lord taught us, and then lists The Lord's prayer. That is a perfect example of a prayer. It addresses the Lord, then praises Him. "Hallowed be thy name. Thy kingdom come, thy will be done..." Next, it asks for a request. "Give us this day our daily bread, and forgive us our sins (our trespasses)." It ends with more praise, "For thine is the kingdom and the power and the glory forever."

The Lord's Prayer

Our Father, who art in Heaven
Hallowed be thy name.
Thy kingdom come, thy will be done
On earth as it is in Heaven.
Give us this day our daily bread
And forgive us our debts as we forgive our debters (or
forgive us our tresspasses as we forgive those who tres-
pass against us)
Lead us not into temptation
But deliver us from evil,
For thine is the kingdom, and the power and the glory
forever.
Amen.
(The Catholic religion drops the last part, but it is basi-
cally the same prayer.)

When you pray to God there is no "right" or
"wrong" way. Sometimes a person feels inadequate
when they try to pray if they aren't use to it. Practice
praying and you will feel more comfortable. A family
can become very close and it can be quite a blessing to
the family if they participate in group prayers. One of
the parents can start and then they go around the circle
with each person adding whatever they want. If someone does not want to do it, they can be passed the first
few times, but after a while it is good to help the person
along. Just to say "God bless us" is something and could
give the person the confidence to begin praying out
loud, adding a little more each time.

"I'm Not Very Good At Praying"

Experience does not makes a difference in prayer. Knowledge of the Bible does not count either. When we pray we are all the same. There is no "good prayer" or no "right" way of doing it.

Coming from the heart in love and sincerity is the only thing that counts. We should avoid setting up a hierarchy in prayer, with priests and ministers on top and the rest of us on bottom. That's not what prayer is all about.

If you stress the role of experience in prayer, this will discourage novice or first-time pray-ers from taking up this practice. We should be encouraging people to pray, not turning them off.
From *Prayer Is Good Medicine* by Larry Dossey, M.D.

Reading Other People's Prayers

Sometimes when we are hurting, the words we yearn for seem far away. It is helpful to read someone else's prayers because it makes you feel you are not alone in your thoughts and feelings. Anyone who is hurting will benefit by reading Marianne Williamson's *Illuminated Prayers*. It is a beautifully decorated book filled with prayers. Just the appearance of the book will cheer a person up.

Mother Teresa often spoke of peace in her talks. If you read her speeches, they are great starts to learning to pray."Let us thank God for the Opportunity He has given us," she says in one speech; then she goes on to pray for peace, joy, and love. In our every day prayer life, these are good things to pray for.

A Prayer For A Sick Child
(can be modified for any sick person)
A Mother's Prayer

Oh Lord, give me the strength I need to deal with the trials you have given me.
Let me understand though reasons may be few.
Lord, let me trust in those who have the knowledge and skill to help. Give them the talent and compassion to know what is best. Above All, Lord, Walk with me as I know you will. Never let me doubt your peace. Please, Lord, help my child be able to be all that she can or wants to be.

A Scared Mother Who Believes

I spotted this prayer surrounded by pictures of a child with various hospital workers in the hall at a hospital I was visiting. It was signed "Baby Carly's Mom, a Scared Mother Who Believes."

That poem was beautiful, but her signature was the inspiration to me. "A Scared Mother Who Believes." We may be scared, but as long as we believe and keep having faith, we will be taken care of. Don't let doubt creep in, just ask the Lord to walk with you and He will. Chances are, he's already walking with you right now.

Praying With The Whole Family

When your children are young, you can gather them together and teach them to pray out loud like this. You can start:

"Thank you God for all of the wonderful blessings you have given us. I am thankful for the beautiful day we had today..."

And then the other adult, if there is one could add:

"I am thankful we are all together,"

Now it is the child's turn.

When they are young and just learning to pray out loud you may get anything and you have to try not to laugh. You could get **"Thank you God for my Legos,"** *and to that you can add,* **"That was very good, it feels good to thank God for all of our blessings. Another thing you can thank God for is that He gave you your eyes to see your Legos and healthy hands to play with them."**

From *Keeping Your Kids Grounded When You're Flying By The Seat Of Your Pants* By Tim Jordan, M.D. and Sally Tippett Rains

Praying Out Loud Can Be Such A Blessing To Everyone In The Prayer Circle

I was leading a Bible Study once and I suggested we go around the circle and pray out loud. Most of the ladies had never prayed out loud and I could tell they were a little apprehensive.

As we went around the circle, you could feel the presence of the Lord in that room and as each woman asked for prayers for very specific things, you could hear the sniffling of the others as they were moved to tears during this prayer.

After it was over, everyone was so thankful that they had prayed out loud. It brings you closer to those you are praying for and it helps you give your burdens to the Lord, but also to the others who are praying with and for you.

Christian Holidays

If you are going through a tough time, the holidays can often be difficult. The best advice I can give on this is "don't blame it on the holidays." If your loved one died around Christmas and loved to celebrate that time of year, then embrace it, don't run from it. Honor your loved one by celebrating, and especially celebrate the true and sacred meaning of the season.

Prayer for Christmas Season...
Dear Lord,
What wonderful blessings you
have given us. Thank you for
being here in our lives, thank you for sending your son to live on earth as a human so we could get to know him on a more personal level.

As this busy season approaches us, may we take the time to see the Christ Child. May we see this baby as the babies we are in our faith. Let each day bring more trust in you O Lord, as we grow in our faith.

Thank you for mothers and fathers that they can care for their children. We are all your children. Thank you, Heavenly Father, that you will hold us in your loving arms and take care of us just as Mary cared for baby Jesus so many years ago.

Help us to appreciate all of the blessings we have, even though our hearts are hurting. Help us to realize you are our only hope. You bring us hope and you never desert us, no matter what our situation is.

Amen

Prayer for Easter...

Dear Lord,

Thank you for the blessings you have given us. Thank you so much that you sent your Son to redeem us. During this holy week, may Thursday bring remembrance, Friday bring reverance, Saturday: realization, and Sunday: Resurrection! Please let us experiece many feelings this week as we prepare our hearts for Easter. Thank you for all of these feelings and in them remind us that You are there for us during all of it...the good, the bad, the sad,...the unexpected and especially....you are with us until the end.

Thank you Lord; thank you for the blessing of life and of family and friends. Thank you for each moment you give us with special friends and family members, no matter how short the time may be. As we begin to see the buds come out and change from one season to another, help us through the seasons of our lives.

Remind us gently always "not to cry because its over, but to smile because it happened."

Thank you Lord for this wonderful day and we praise you as you give us grace. Amen.

Reading the Psalms Is A Good Way To Pray.

The book of Psalms is full of religious poetry. If you take out your Bible and look at the book of Psalms you will see there are hymns of praise and adoration, as well as thanksgiving and lamentations. Psalms I and 37 have been called "Wisdom Poetry."

Psalm I
Happy are those
Who do not follow the advice
Of the wicked,
Or take the path that sinners tread,
Or sit in the seat of scoffers;
But their delight is in the law of the Lord,
And on his law they meditate day and night.
They are like trees
Planted by streams of water,
Which yield their fruit in its season,
And their leaves do not wither.
In all that they do, they prosper.

The wicked are not so,
But are like chaff that the wind
Drives away.
Therefore the wicked will not
Stand in the judgment,
Nor sinners in the congregation of the righteous;
For the Lord watches over the way of the righteous,
But the way of the wicked will perish.

"I'm Not Comfortable Praying...How Can I Get Started?"

Using the Psalms as a basis for starting your prayer life can be very helpful. Whenever we pray to God, we should always start by thanking him. No matter how bad your life has gotten in your eyes, there is always something to thank God for. Look outside, if it is a beautiful day, you can thank Him for the day. If the weather is bad in your eyes, you can thank Him you have eyes to see it with, or you can thank Him you have ears to hear the weather report. There is always something you can thank God for. Look to the Psalms to help with praising and thanking God.

One of the most obvious effects of the psalmists' vision of God is the call to prayers of adoration, praise and thanksgiving. For it was that vision which led them to give the whole world some of the most magnificent words of adoration ever uttered. And when, after more then 2,000 years, we strive for words which express our sense of wonder and awe in the presence of God, we find ourselves pouring forth the words of the psalmists. They have taught us to adore God, to praise God, and to be filled with gratitude to God.

Mack B. Stokes in *Talking With God*

Using a "Thy will be done" or "May the best thing happen" approach in prayer requires faith and trust that the best outcome will prevail. It also means setting aside our preferences and demands. This can be difficult, because most of us feel we know in advance what's best, and we waste no time in the Absolute what to do.

From *Prayer Is Good Medicine* by Larry Dossey, M.D

"...Even though we do not have the answers, He does. He has perfect timing for all things in our lives." Joyce Meyer

"I don't understand fully how prayer works, or why it would make a difference to the creator of the universe what I say! But, I have learned the importance of obedience and God tells us to pray without ceasing."

Dr. Debra Peppers, in *It's Your Turn*

Prayer Has Incredible Power

Debra Peppers, a member of the National Teachers Hall of Fame and a thirty year educator with a Ph.D decided one day to give up her secure job as a drama teacher at a high school to embark on a speaking career. Her whole goal is to spread tne great news that she knows from personal experience and that is that no situation is too big for God to handle.

Debra went through a period during her younger years where she was a lost soul. She became involved in drugs, lost interest in school, ran away, and even considered suicide. But somewhere in there she summmoned up the faith that had been rooted in her heart by her parents. She credits a teacher she calls "Miss Alma" as the one who actually helped her see that the Lord was the only way out of her misery.

In her book, *It's Your Turn Now* (available through www.pepperseed.org) she encourages prayer and has come up with this anacronym:

P raise
R epent
A sk
Y ourself

Through the power of prayer, Debra Peppers went from a high school drop out who was 100 pounds overweight to a national speaker with her own radio show, who has spoken at Robert Shuller's Crystal Cathederal. Her message also includes the attitude of "If I can do it...so can you!"

We can. We don't all have to be national speakers or in the Hall of Fame, but we can learn from someone who achieves success and then makes it her mission to lift others up.

Prayer really does work. It works in strange and often unknown ways. There are some people who go through a tragedy and think God has forgotten about them; that their prayers were not answered. God never forgets about you, he just may have something different in mind for you than you thought.

Jabez's Prayer

Recently the prayer of Jabez has become very popular because an author explained it in a book. When people saw how simple it was, it attracted many readers. The verse can be found in Chronicles 4:10

"Jabez cried out to the God of Israel, 'Oh, that you would bless me and enlarge my territory! Let your hand be with me, and keep me from harm so that I will be free from pain.' And God granted his request."

The prayer is a bold one: Jabez asked God for exactly what he wanted and God gave it to him. Though it may be bold, it is not selfish; it is biblical. It is the type of prayer that according to God's word in the Bible, is what God intends us to pray.

Chapter Nine
The Bible As A Source
Of Peace

One of my favorite quotations regarding Christianity came from a man I have respected for many years. Gene Stallings is a famous football coach and I came to know him when he coached the St. Louis Cardinals (now known as Arizona Cardinals).

"I don't know the Scriptures as well as some," he said, "but I know that being a Christian doesn't mean that you're not going to have some trials along the way. Faith is realizing there is going to be some bad that comes along with the good."

There are two reasons I like that quote, the first being that Stallings admits he doesn't know all of the Bible verses. Sometimes we can become intimidated by people who constantly quote scripture and this can cause us to feel inferior to them; like they are better Christians.

There are no "better Christians." Once we become Christians we are Christians because of the grace God has given us, not because of how hard we try. This has been something I always struggled with. I worked so hard at trying to be a good Christian because I wanted to be sure I made it to Heaven.

Maybe that is how you feel right now, you need the Lord, but you are afraid maybe you don't deserve His love or that you haven't been a "good enough" Christian. Maybe you are afraid to pray because you don't know the "right" words.

Like Gene Stallings said, "being a Christian doesn't mean that you're not going to have some trials along the way." We just have to keep our faith that throughout the good and the bad times, the Lord will always be with us. Don't be afraid to pray. God hears the prayers of someone who says, "God, if you're up there, hey man, I need help. It stinks what's happening and I can't do it alone. I need ya man."

He doesn't care if you don't use polished English or if you are not down on your knees in prayer. The Lord is there for you and He wants you to come to Him. He's waiting, just like a parent who wants to help her child.

In his book, *The Purpose Driven Life*, Rick Warren offers a way to pray throughout the day. He calls it "breath prayers."

"You choose a brief sentence or a simple phrase that can be repeated to Jesus in one breath: 'You are with me.' 'I receive your grace.' 'I'm depending on you.' 'I want to know you.' 'I belong to you.' 'Help me trust you.'"

Warren also says you can use a favorite scripture in this way. I always say "He will keep in perfect peace, all who trust him, whose thoughts turn often to the Lord." It is a great verse from the book of Isaiah and it comes in very handy.

If you use a "breath prayer" in good times, they will be there for you in bad times. When you most need a prayer, it will pop into your head.

Thanks And Praise

Psalm 100:1
Make a joyful noise to the Lord, all the earth. Worship the Lord with gladness; coming into his presence with singing.

Isaiah 12:1
You will say in that day: I will give thanks to you, O Lord, for though you were angry with me, your anger turned away and you comforted me.

Isaiah 12:5
Sing praises to the Lord for He has done gloriously. Let this be known in all the earth. Shout aloud and sing for joy, O Royal Zion, for great in your midst is the Holy One of Israel.

Psalm 100:4
Enter his gates with thanksgiving, and his courts with praise. Give thanks to him, bless his name.

Psalm 108:1-4
My heart is steadfast, o God, my heart is steadfast; I will sing and make melody. Awake, my soul! Awake, O harp and lyre! I will awake the dawn. I will give thanks to you, O Lord, among the peoples, and I will sing praises to you among the nations. For your steadfast love is higher than the heavens, and your faithfulness reaches to the clouds.

For Comfort

Philippians 4:6,7
Don't worry about anything; instead, pray about everything; tell God your needs and don't forget to thank him for his answers. If you do this you will experience God's peace, which is far more wonderful than the human mind can understand. His peace will keep your thoughts and your hearts quiet and at rest as you trust in Christ Jesus.

1 Peter 5:7
Let Him have all your worries and cares, for He is always thinking about you and watching everything that concerns you.

John 14:27
I am leaving you with a gift--peace of mind and heart! And the peace I give isn't fragile like the peace the world gives. So don't be troubled or afraid.

2 Corinthians 4:16-18
This is why we never give up. Though our bodies are dying, our inner strength in the Lord is growing every day. These troubles and sufferings of ours are, after all, quite small and won't last very long. Yet this short time of distress will result in God's richest blessings upon us forever and ever! So we do not look at what we can see right now, the troubles all around us, but we look forward to the joys in Heaven which we have not yet seen. The troubles will soon be over, but the joys to come will last forever.

Psalms 65:5
By awesome deeds you answer us with deliverance. O God of our salvation; you are the hope of all the earth and of the farthest seas.

1 Peter 3:10
For those who desire life and desire to see good days, let them keep their tongues from evil and their lips from speaking deceit; let them turn away from evil and do good; let them seek peace and pursue it. For the eyes of the Lord are on the righteous and his ears are open to their prayer. But the face of the Lord is against those who do evil.

Psalm 109: 32
For I am poor and needy, and my heart is pierced within me. I am gone like a shadow at evening; I am shaken off like a locust. My knees are weak through fasting, my body has become gaunt. I am an object of scorn to my accusers; when they see me they shake their fists.
Help me, O Lord my God! Save me according to your steadfast love.

If You Are Suffering

Psalm 46:1-3
God is our refuge and strength, a very present help in trouble. Therefore we will not fear though the earth should change, though the mountains shake in the heart of the sea; though its waters roar and foam, though the mountains tremble with tumult.

John 16:33B
Be of good cheer, I have overcome the world.

John 14:2
In my Father's house are many rooms; if it were not so, would I have told you that I go to prepare a place for you?

Proverbs 3:5-6
Trust in the Lord with all your heart and do not rely on your own insight. In all your ways acknowledge Him and He will make straight your paths.

2 Corinthians 4:16
So we do not lose heart. Even though our outer nature is wasting away, our inner nature is being renewed day by day. For this slight momentary affliction is preparing us for an eternal weight of glory beyond all measure, because we look not at what can be seen but at what cannot be seen; for what can be seen is temporary, but what cannot be seen is eternal.

If You Are Tempted To Sin

1 Corinthians 10:13
But remember this--the wrong desires that come into your life aren't anything new and different. Many others have faced exactly the same problems before you. And no temptation is irresistible. You can trust God to keep the temptation from becoming so strong that you can't stand up against it, for He has promised this and will do what he says. He will show you how to escape temptation's power so that you can bear up patiently against it.

Proverbs 3:21
My child, do not let these escape from your sight: keep sound wisdom and prudence, and they will be life for your soul and adornment for your neck. Then you will walk on your way securely and your foot will not stumble.

Lamentations 3:25
The Lord is good to those who wait for Him, to the soul that seeks Him.

Romans 12:9
Let love be genuine; hate what is evil, hold fast to what is good; love one another with mutual affection; out do one another in showing honor.

Financial Problems

Hebrews 13:5

Stay away from the love of money; be satisfied with what you have. For God has said, "I will never, never fail you nor forsake you."

Matthew 6: 24-34

You cannot serve two masters: God and money. For you will hate one and love the other, or else the other way around.

So my counsel is: Don't worry about *things*-food, drink, and clothes. For you already have life and a body-and they are far more important than what to eat and wear. Look at the birds! They don't worry about what to eat--they don't need to sow or reap or store up food--for your Heavenly Father feeds them. And you are far more valuable to Him than they are. Will all your worries add a single moment to your life?

And why worry abour your clothes? Look at the field lilies! They don't worry about theirs. Yet King Solomon in all his glory was not clothed as beautifully as they. And if God cares so wonderfully for flowers that are here today and gone tomorrow, won't he more surely care for you, O men of little faith?

So don't worry at all about having enough food and clothing. Why be like the heathen? For they take pride in all these things and are deeply concerned about them. But your Heavenly Father already knows perfectly well that you need them and He will give them to you if you give Him first place in your life and live as he wants you to.

So don't be anxious about tomorrw. God will take care of your tomorrow too. Live one day at a time.

Romans 12:12
Rejoice in hope, be patient in suffering, persevere in prayer.

1 Peter 4:12
Beloved, do not be surprised at the fiery ordeal that is taking place among you to test you, as though something strange were happening to you. But rejoice insofar as you are sharing Christ's sufferings, so that you may also be glad and shout for joy when his glory is revealed.

God will see you through your problems, even the scary financial ones.

Need To Trust God in Times of Adversity

Psalms 3
O Lord how many are my foes!
Many are rising against me;
Many are saying to me,
"There is no help for you in God"
But you, O Lord are a shield around me,
My glory, and the one who
Lifts up my head.
I cry aloud to the Lord and
He answers me from his holy hill.
I lie down and sleep;
I wake again, for the Lord
Sustains me.
I am not afraid of ten thousands
Of people
Who have set themselves against me all around.
Rise up, O Lord!
Deliver me O my God!
For you strike all my enemies on the cheek;
You break the teeth of the wicked.
Deliverance belongs to the Lord;
May your blessings be on your people.

Psalms 67
May God be gracious to us and bless us and make his
face to shine upon us.

Ephesians 4:14
For this reason I bow my knees before the Father, from whom every family in heaven and on earth takes its name. I pray that according to the riches of his glory, he may grant that you may be strengthened in your inner being with power through his Spirit and that Christ may dwell in your hearts through faith, as you are being rooted and grounded in love.

Romans 12:14-19
Bless those who persecute you; bless and do not curse them. Rejoice with those who rejoice, weep with those who weep. Live in harmony with one another; do not be haughty, but associate with the lowly; do not claim to be wiser than you are. Do not repay anyone evil for evil, but take thought for what is noble in the sight of all. If it is possible, so far as it depends on you, live peaceably with all.

Revelations 22:12
See I am coming soon; my reward is with me, to repay according to everyone's work. I am the Alpha and the Omega, the first and the last, the beginning and the end.

Need Help With Self Esteem----Feel Worthless

Psalms 139: 14-16
I praise you, for I am fearfully and wonderfully made.
Wonderful are your works; that I know very well. My
frame was not hidden from you, when I was being made
in secret, intricately woven in the depths of the earth.
Your eyes beheld my unformed substance. In your book
were written all the days that were formed for me when
none of them as yet existed.

John 17:24
Father, I desire that those also, whom you have given
me, may be with me where I am, to see my glory which
you have given me because you loved me before the
foundation of the world.

Jeremiah 31:3
I have loved you with an everlasting love; therefore I
have continued my faithfulness to you. Again I will
build you and you shall be built.

Ephesians 1:11-12
In Christ we have also obtained an inheritance, having been destined according to the purpose of him who accomplishes all things according to his counsel and will, so that we, who were the first to set our hope on Christ, might live for the praise of his glory.

Genesis 1:27
So God created humankind in his image,
In the image of God He created them;
Male and female he created them.

Ephesians 6:10
Finally, be strong in the Lord and in the strength of his power. Put on the whole armor of God so that you may be able to stand against the wiles of the devil.

Chapter Ten

The Words of Respected Figures

Reading the words and quotations of people we admire can give us the right words for a certain situation. There are just some lines that never go out of style even though they don't have any significant meaning. "I never met a man I didn't like," will forever be Will Rogers. You can't hear the words, "Come up and see me sometime!" and not think of May West; and of course, "There's no place like home!" is Judy Garland as she played Dorothy in the Wizard of Oz.

The following quotations are from famous people, but the quotation itself may not be recognizable. Whether you like the person or don't, their sentiments are worth reading.

Jack Buck (Hall of Fame Broadcaster)

Things turn out for the best for those who make the best of the way things turn out.

Carole (his wife) once asked me what I would say if I met the Lord, and my answer then is the same as it is now: I want to ask Him why He was so good to me.

Pope John Paul

Don't Be Afraid.

As the world was on the verge of a new millenium, many people were fearful. There was the threat of the "Y2K Virus" where every computer would fail just as midnight passed. If that would have happened, people were afraid they might not be able to have enough food, and there would be much uncertainty. Some even feared the world would end at midnight. Suddenly a joyful occasion, the dawn of a new year had turned into a terrorizing thought for many people.

The Pope delivered his New Years message and he used the words of Jesus Christ himself as he tried to calm the fearful. The Pope's words on the dawn of the Millenium reminded us, "Don't be afraid."

Just those three simple words can bring about such a peaceful feeling in themselves. Whether a person is Catholic or not does not matter when the Pope spoke. He was trying to comfort all people. Many times in the Bible the phrase 'don't be afraid' was used or paraphrased. Before Jesus' birth when the people were afraid of what was happening, the angel Gabriel came down and said 'Fear not for I bring you tidings of great joy, that unto you tonight in the city of David, a Saviour will be born...'

Sometimes when you are afraid, just envisioning the Pope in all his peacefulness saying "Don't be afraid," can calm you down.

Dale Carnegie

Don't be afraid to give your best to what seemingly are small jobs. Every time you conquer one it makes you that much stronger. If you do the little jobs well, the big ones tend to take care of themselves.

Take a chance! All life is a chance. The man who goes the furthest is generally the one who is willing to do and dare. The sure thing boat never gets far from shore.

Thomas Jefferson

Nothing on earth can stop the man with the right mental attitude from achieving his goals; nothing on earth can help the man with the wrong mental attitude.

Ozzie Smith

It (success) is pretty simple. You work hard. Perseverance, dedication, courage, the intestinal fortitude to be the best you can be, those are the keys not only to my success but to anybody's. You've got to be willing to go the extra mile. You've got to be willing to sacrifice.

There has to be some blood, some sweat and some tears. There is no success without them. That is really the key: being able to put your head in there and grind it out. Every day is not going to be a great day. Having that desire to grind and work through your problems and learn from them is what being successful is all about.

Norman Vincent Peale

You only lose energy when life becomes dull in your mind. Your mind gets bored and therefore tired of doing nothing. Get interested in something! Get absolutely enthralled in something! Get out of yourself! Be somebody! Do something. The more you lose yourself in something bigger than yourself, the more energy you will have.

John F. Kennedy

We should not let our fears hold us back from pursuing our hopes.

The courage of life is often a less dramatic spectacle than the courage of the final moment; but it is no less a magnificent mixture of triumph and tragedy. A man does what he must-in spite of personal consequences; in spite of obstacles and dangers and pressures-and that is the basis of all morality.

Ronald Reagan

I'm convinced more than ever that man finds liberation only when he binds himself to God and commits himself to his fellow man.

Dr. Martin Luther King Jr.

One day we must come to see that peace is not merely a distant goal we seek, but that it is a means by which we arrive at that goal. We must pursue peaceful ends through peaceful means.

Take the first step in faith. You don't have to see the whole staircase, just take the first step.

Helen Keller

Be of good cheer. Do not think of today's failures, but of the success that may come tomorrow. You have set yourself a difficult task, but you will succeed if you persevere; and you will find a joy in overcoming obstacles.

Although the world is full of suffering, it is also full of the overcoming of it.

Eleanor Roosevelt

He who loses money, loses much; He who loses a friend, loses much more, He who loses faith, loses all.

Chapter 11
Motivational Poetry

Need Some Inspiration:

It Couldn't Be Done
Edgar A. Guest

Somebody said that it couldn't be done,
  But he with a chuckle replied
That "maybe it couldn't," but he would be one
  Who wouldn't say so till he'd tried.
So he buckled right in with the trace of a grin
  On his face. If he worried he hid it.
He started to sing as he tackled the thing
  That couldn't be done, and he did it.

There are thousands to tell you it cannot be done,
  There are thousands to prophesy failure;
There are thousands to point out to you, one by one,
  The dangers that wait to assail you.
But just buckle in with a bit of a grin,
  Just take off your coat and go to it;
Just start to sing as you tackle the thing
  That "cannot be done," and you'll do it.

Who Can Be Against You?

I woke up early this morning
I found a place to pray.
Nothing's going to come first
Besides the Lord, my God today.

The verse in Romans says
He's for me, He's on my side.
Then if that's true and I know it is
No one can be against me though they've tried.

For I have got my armor.
My protection from the bad.
And all I've got to do is just
Be in His world and just be glad.

If each new day you put Him first
You fill your heart with the Lord
Then there's no room inside you for bad things
You're protected like a sword.

You may want peace and guidance
Away from all the noise.
If you spend time with God
Then you will know His voice.

Morning Meeting

In a few short minutes the phone will ring
The kids will wake up and start everything.
I've quietly made it to this special place
I sit with my candles, a smile on my face.

My Bible is close, my prayer book is near
During these moments the Lord God is here.
I know He is with me throughout the day
In these private moments I ask Him to show me the way.

Help me to greet the day happy and not come unglued.
Help me to speak kindly, not mean and rude.
If the kids make me mad, may I answer them sweetly
Please, Dear Lord come into my heart, completely.

When the stress of the world tries to get the best of me
May this moment with you, God, help set me free.
Help keep me more gently, more loving and giving.
Thank you Lord for our time and this living.

Thank you that I know you will make me ok.
Thank you for taking those heavy weights of worry
away.
Thanks that you share my burdens and fears.
Thanks for being with me all of these years.

Just a few private moments, a few little prayers
And I know I will be ok, I know my Lord cares.
It's lovely here, so peaceful and still.
He's never deserted me and He never will.

When All You Can Do Is Pray

When the worry comes as it sometimes will
I go and find someplace quiet and still.
I light it up with a candle or two
And say to the Lord, "I give it up to you."

For sometimes it seems all you can do is pray
When the problems seem so large and gray.
When there seems to be no solution in sight
Don't give up because God just might...

Have an idea you haven't come up with yet
And He might have a thought that you haven't met.
When you are alone in the night with bad dreams
Things aren't always as bad as it seems.

God will stay by you no matter how bad the season
He's called the 'Savior' for a reason.
So give it up to God on that worrisome day
Because sometimes all you can do is pray.

Driving Through Fog

Driving through fog is difficult
It seems impossible..like there's no way out
But there are three ways out ...
You can stop in the middle
because you are gripped with fear
Give up and stop.
A large truck could come upon your stopped car and
smash you.
You could pull over and wait the fog out.
Fog always lifts after a time.
Or you can keep going and look for a set of car lights
ahead to follow.
When you see those lights just drive safely following the
light and soon
you will be out of the fog.
That choice is the best but it
Requires effort on your part.
If you try, you can do it.
The same is true in our lives.
Sometimes it seems like our problems are insurmount-
able or it's like we are walking around in a fog.
Take the third choice.
Look for a light. Focus on what's good in your life.
Work to find that light and
Soon you will be driving through safely.

Enjoy This Day

Have you every noticed how
When times are rough
If you live for 'this day'
Then 'this day' is enough.

When the worries ahead seem
Too hard to bear
Then live for today
And today you are there.

And as you live in this day
Break it down by the hour
And then by the minute
And you'll soon feel its power.

When it all seems so hard
When times are most tense
Those are the days when
We need common sense.

If you're worried about
A loved one's health
Don't let it bring you down every day
Enjoy what you have, enjoy your wealth.

Maybe some day
The worst will come true.
But worrying right now
What good does it do?

It only will make this
Short, precious time
(That you could have enjoyed them)
Be gone--what a crime.

And if by chance it turns out as it should
Turns out in your favor
You wasted your time worrying
The time you should savor.

You're uncertain of what
The next day will bring
And though you don't like life's concert
You might as well sing.

Soon you will realize
That nothing is neater
When you live for each moment
You life is much sweeter.

You're Still Here

Life goes on as it always does
And I'm right there in life because
There are things to do that must be done
And it doesn't do any good to run.

A part of me is missing
And I now know it is you.
It always seems so trite to say
That "you're a part of me"
But ever since you left there's been a hole I see.

It's a funny feeling I can't explain
And it feels a little worse when the weather is rain.
I go about my business but when there's a pause
I get a funny feeling…that's one of my flaws.

It hasn't been right
I can't say quite why
But so often the smallest thing
Will make me cry.

But then in my mind, I see your smiling face
And suddenly I am filled with Grace.
And I thank God for the time that we had
And suddenly I am feeling glad.

For our time together was a precious gift from God
And though you are gone and it feels odd,
Your warmth is inside me and you guide me along
And this feeling you are with me I know is not wrong.

So thank you for sharing sunshine & happy times with me
Thanks for the times that you made "you" and
"me"…We.
I thank God for every blessing given to me from Above.
And I especially thank God that I had you to love.

Lipstick Makes You Look Happy

Lipstick is a wonderful thing,
It makes your face all bright
And a little dab of blush
Makes you look just right.

Comb your hair and
Put on your smile and
No one will notice you've
Been blue for a while.

This is a trick from my mother
She's graceful and very strong
When ever you see her she's shining
And you can't tell that something's wrong.

Under her colorful face, and
 Smile so happy and fake,
She's worried about this, or fearful about that,
But she keeps smiling for goodness sake.

And then a strange and wonderful thing
Begins to actually take place
She forgets that she's worried and begins to cheer up
From the smile she sees on my face.

For whenever you spread your light around
Others will join in the game
And soon those around you will cheer you up
And you'll be laughing again, just the same.

If I Were a Flower
What Kind of Flower Would I Be?
By Nancy Tippett

I am a little plastic flower in the Queen's hat.
All the other flowers in her hat are blue silk,
But the crafty hat maker has played a shabby trick on the Queen
And placed with great care
One solitary blue plastic flower among the silk!

I love being the one who is different and have a more permanent
shape.
When the Queen tires of her hat and puts it away in her closet
All the other flowers will turn from a powder blue to a steel blue
And eventually a drab gray, but not me.
I will forever be a beautiful powder blue daisy
Perhaps the only one in existence on the whole planet.
And when the Queen dies and her things are given to the poor
people,
An old woman will be so pleased to have such a hat
With dozens of gray silk flowers and one beautiful blue shining
daisy.

As the hat eventually grows old, she will pluck out her favorite
And toss away the rest of the hat and draw a picture of me
And then paint me on her favorite piece of china.
I will be immortalized then,
And perhaps given to the Queen as a gift from a pauper.
And the Queen won't know what a special flower I am,
But she will eat off me for the rest of her days.

Mother's Hands

The beautiful hands--nails polished all pink
There's nothing prettier than her hands I used to think.
I'd file my nails and polish with color and clear
So I could look as graceful as my mother so dear.

Those hands that combed my curls with care
Turned the steering wheel as she drove us everywhere.
They scolded me when my manners flew by
And they hugged me close when I started to cry.

Now I'm a mom and I can't forget
How she held the dryer when my hair was wet.
Now I have colorful nails and rings
And I too wear jewelry and other things.

My Mother's hands shake today
When she goes to write or eat or pray
And lines are there that once were not
She still wears the polish like when I was a tot.

The rings are there--jewelry so nice
I wouldn't trade that sight for any price.
Those hands that were always here for me
So nice and pretty for all to see.

They're special and I look at them each chance I get
They're strength and comfort I'll not forget.
When she reaches out as a problem prevails
I take her hands with those pretty nails.

I look down at those lovely hands
Life can be tough, so many demands
Through all the laughter and the tears
I've been blessed to know her for all these years.

You're Worth It

Don't judge your worth by what others say.
It's time you realized how important you are today.
No one person should be in control of you.
Stay in touch with God, and you'll know what to do.

If you are feeling trapped--can't do the things you want
Don't sit and watch it happen--if you can't hit at least
try to bunt!
The Lord doesn't want you to suffer at the hands of a
selfish boar.
He wants the lion and lamb to both be able to roar.

The Lord has made you perfect--He puts you to a test.
He wants you to realize you have grace, and settle for
nothing less.
Ask the Lord what He wants from you, where His heart
is at.
And never settle for second best, you're too good for
that.

The New Year

Today is a new day, I want you all to hear
I'll treat it like it's January 1--the first day of the year.
I'll do the things I want--The things I dream about.
Instead of pitying myself, I'll actually break out.

Nobody can keep me down, I'm way too good you see.
The Lord gave me butterfly wings to fly
And even though I wonder why
I know he wants me to go and try
To be the best I can be.

So with each new day and dawn
I'll put my best face on.
And ask the Lord to help me
As I step out on the lawn

I'll face the day with hope
Never from his light will I shift
Today is my chance to start anew
Today is a special gift.

At the Hospital

Beep, beep, beep
There's a strange silence here,
You are softly breathing and
There is beep, beep, beep.
So different to see you
'hooked up.'
Wires here, wires there.
Lights on the machine.
You stir.
Weakly you smile at me.
That smile was worth a million dollars.
I feel better already.
You are the one sick
But you just made me feel better.
For the last five hours
It was just you, me, and the Lord.
Thank the Lord, He was here.
Or it would have been just you and me...
And you were asleep.
That beep, beep, beep could scare a person.
But you smiled at me.
Thank you. Lord. for that smile.

Healing

She said she was well, she knew she was
And the grown-ups were happy, they smiled because
They knew what the doctors said, that she still had the cancer
But she said she was well, this tiny dancer.

And several months later the grown-ups were thrilled
The MRI was clear on this girl so strong-willed.
She knew she was healed, the Lord said it was true
And she started to live like a healed person would do.

May you keep the faith of a child in your heart
May you find the scriptures of comfort, and part
With your grown-up ways and your grown-up fears
May the Lord replace them with happy tears.

Waiting On Test Results

We just got home from the taking some tests
The doctors and nurses are on a quest
To find out what is wrong with you
And we sure want to know it, too.

Things just don't seem quite right with you
And you know you don't feel like you usually do
The tests will help the docs figure out
What's really wrong, so there isn't a doubt.

There's just one problem in waiting for tests
They might turn out bad or they might be the best.
There's such a small distance between malignant and
benign.
One day you're fine…it's just a thin line.

I'm asking God to make the tests say 'no'
I want you to go home and play in the snow.
I'm praying for a clean reading…that nothing is there
I'm praying so hard, Lord, hear my prayer.

And if it's God's will that there is a tumor
If it turns out the truth is no rumor,
Then I'm praying God's peace will be on us all
I'm praying for calmness if we get a bad call.

For no matter what the doctors say,
(And a bad diagnosis could not be crueler)
I know in my heart
That God is the ruler.

With God, all things are not as they seem
With God, we have the capacity to dream.
We should never accept the worst thing that they say
Hold on to hope, hold on, every day.

Never give up, keep your faith in the Lord.
Never let your positive attitude ever become bored.
Don't give up, to failure, say, "nope"
And never, never, ever give up the hope.

May God bless your heart for the fear that you feel
May God know your heart and your faith is for real.
May peace be your comfort as you wait, may you rest
May God be with you when you hear the results of the
test.

Worry

Yesterday was a scary day
Tomorrow might be one too
But today I'm basking in my happiness
We got a little good news about you.

It seems I'm always worried
Will you be ok or will you not?
I remember the fun we used to have
But then sometimes I forgot.

I forgot to give my worries
To the Lord above to keep.
On those worrisome days,
Those nights I don't get much sleep.

You mean the world to me
I wish my worries would cease.
I try to go on, but the fear is so much
Oh, God, won't you please give me peace.

Peace is the gift we can all get.
If we will just let the Lord know our fears.
In the moment you least expect it.
He'll be there to dry all your tears.

So never give up,
Don't accept the worst news.
Just keep faith in the Lord
And you never can lose.

Divorce

How long does it take one heart to mend?
What causes a 'perfect' marriage to end?
These are questions as through life we wander
These are questions a mother must ponder.

To see a friend or loved one's divorce
Is very upsetting and sad, of course
But when that person is a daughter or son
It hurts to think they are the one.

At first it seems like such a shock
It's like it's not happening, not on the clock.
But then as the reality sets in with the strife
You know it will affect the rest of their life.

But only the two can know for sure
If saving the marriage has no cure
It's not for another to second guess
They didn't have to live in the mess.

So all you can do is pray for your child
And hope that the repercussions will all be mild.
God knows the answer and will help them all through
If you'll ask Him, he'll even give comfort to you.

For sometimes it's better to fail at a thing
That will ultimately succeed and peace it will bring.
For to succeed at something that will ultimately fail
Is hanging on by the end of a tail.

Let it go, if go it must,
The memories may turn to silver from rust.
And life can go on for both of the two
And it goes on for the rest of the family, too.

A family is something that never will end
By law it may change but if nurtured, my friend
A family can survive almost anything it sees
And the members grow stronger with new family trees.

The Box

I am in a box
My box is see-through, it's glass
or maybe ice, because it's sometimes cold.
No one else is in my box, but sometimes
someone else is very close, that's why I think
it might be ice. Because on some days it almost melts.
In my box, tears come when they want to, my temper
flares easily,
and I sometimes pull the covers over my box so no
one will see me and I won't have to see anyone.
If there was a mirror in my box I would turn it around
so I won't see myself
The box has made me look old, the box has made me
so wrapped up in the walls that I forgot to take care of
myself. I look fat.
But sometimes I remember when I was just out there.
(Where everything was pretty and free.)
Not in a box, with people thinking 'she's different now'
'She's in a box.'
I remember when it was a warm sunshiny day
 and I felt the hot sun on my shoulders, and it was nice.
I think you are in a box too, and maybe if we keep our
boxes real close, then on the days when the walls almost
melt,
We will be close and we can hold hands.

It Hasn't Been A 'Bad' Year

You should never remember time by years
As a 'great' year in smiles and a 'bad' year in tears.
For each new day is a blessing you make
For the way that you live and the chances you take.

Each day is a chance to make a new start
But you've got to reach way down in your heart
And find that enthusiasm that life can give
Then you'll live the life that you were meant to live.

Don't ever look back and wish you'd done 'this'
Or wish you'd done 'that'…what fun you would miss.
Be there in your life and live each day as new
This is my special wish for you.

Never Say Impossible

Never Say 'impossible.' for that's a word I despise.
Just think you can do it, and say you can do it
And others won't see your disguise.
When people try telling you give up it won't work
Then that's when you climb in and
Give it a jerk.
Impossible's a word for losers and such
A word for people who don't care too much.
Just give it a try with a positive spin
And soon you'll accomplish your chore
And you'll win.

It is fun to read poetry out loud.

Poetry Is Magic

Poetry is a wonderful thing. You can read poems and find comfort in them. Another thing you can do is memorize them. When my grandma was in the hospital, my grandpa had a lot of time on his hands. He would read books and poetry. Though he was a senior citizen, he never let his mind rest, and during one of her long hospital stays he taught himself the poem, *Casey at the Bat*. He could also recite by memory the great poem by Robert W. Service, *The Cremation of Sam McGee*.

It is fun to memorize poetry, but sometimes you can't concentrate when your mind is racing. That is when poetry is just a great thing to read. It is easy to read, much shorter than a book.

Chapter Twelve
Prayers And Prayerful Thoughts For All Of Us

Prayer is a special thing. There are many ways to pray, out loud, to yourself, in a group.

The power of prayer is enormous. Prayers can lead to miracles. Praying for a friend or with a friend can bring you closer together. There is a special bond between two people who have prayed together.

Prayer in marriage is like a secret weapon. If things go wrong, it is a blessing to be able to say to your spouse, "Let's pray about it together."

The old saying "the family that prays together stays together" still holds true today. If you are going through a tough time as a family, praying about it together can bring about change and healing.

When all you can do is pray...Try these prayers...

Dear Lord,
I thank you for everything you have given me...all of the wonderful blessings. I thank you for this day, and the living things around me, the beauty of nature and the splendor of the outdoors.

I praise your holy name for all of the great things that have happened to me...the many things I have taken for granted...the many times you have been right here with me when I have needed you.

Now I call out to you in my time of need and I ask you to help me. I have such a problem that I can't figure any way out of it. I can't figure out what I am going to do. All I can do is pray, oh Lord, and all I can do is trust that you will hear my prayer and be with me as I face this terrible thing that is troubling me.

I have faith in you, Lord and I know that is enough. I give my burdens to you and I know that you will ease the heavy load these burdens are causing me. You are a loving God, you have never forsaken me, and I know you never will.

I thank you in advance for helping me through this. I thank you for helping those I love through it also. Just talking to you gives me peace. AMEN

Psalm 61

Hear my cry, O God;
  Listen to my prayer.
From the end of the earth I call
  To you
When my heart is faint.
Lead me to the rock
  That is higher than I;
For you are my refuge
  A strong tower against the enemy.
Let me abide in your tent
  Forever,
Find refuge under the shelter
  Of your wings.
For you, O God, have heard my
  Vows;
  You have given me the
Heritage of those who fear
  Your name.
Prolong the life of the king;
May his years endure to all generations!
May he be enthroned forever before God;
Appoint steadfast love and
Faithfulness to watch over Him!
So I will always sing praises to your name,
As I pay my vows day after day.

Dear Lord,
Come into my heart today and fill me with your goodness and your hope.
Amen

Psalm 18 1-3
I love you, O Lord, my strength.
The Lord is my rock, my fortress, and my deliverer,
My God, my rock in whom I take refuge,
My shield and the horn of my
Salvation, my stronghold.
I call upon the Lord, who is worthy to be praised, so
I shall be saved from my enemies.

Psalm 22:1-5
My God, my God, why have you forsaken me?
Why are you so far from
Helping me, from the words of my groaning?
O my God, I cry by day, but you do not answer;
And by night, but find no rest.

Yet you are holy,
Enthroned on the praises of Israel.
In you our ancestors trusted;
They trusted, and you delivered them.
To you they cried and were saved.
In you they trusted and were not put to shame.

Dear Lord,

Thank you for looking out for me today. You see into my heart, so you know that today I am having a hard day. Things are reminding me of my special loved one that I am missing. I was going along just fine and then "whamo!" the thoughts came and the tears flowed. I am torn because I want to "get over it" but then again I never want to be "over it."

I feel so lonely and sad, but then I see her smiling face in my mind. How lucky I was! But it wasn't luck, you chose me, Lord to be lucky enough to have her in my life. I know you have so much in store for me; that your plan is perfect even though I don't understand it. I know it will be revealed to me some-day, on that great day when we reunite. Thank you for being here with me when I need you. Amen

Psalm 25: 1-10

To you, O Lord, I lift up my soul.
O my God, in you I trust;
Do not let me be put to shame;
Do not let my enemies exult over me.
Do not let those who wait for you be put to shame;
Let them be ashamed who are wantonly treacherous.

Make me to know your ways,
O Lord;
Teach me your paths.
Lead me in your truth, and teach me
For you are the God of my salvation;
For you I wait all day long.

Be mindful of your mercy,
O Lord, and of your steadfast love,
For they have been from of old.
Do not remember the sins of my youth or my transgres-
sions;
According to your steadfast love remember me
For your goodness sake, O Lord!

Good and upright is the Lord;
Therefore he instructs sinners in the way.
He leads the humble in what is right
And teaches the humble His way.
All the paths of the Lord are
Steadfast love and faithfulness,
For those who keep his covenant and his decrees.

When You Need A Prayer...

Reading the Psalms is a good way to pray. There are prayers for all occasions in the Psalms. They are beautiful, like poems. Sometimes when we pray, we are praying for something specific and when things don't turn out the way we wanted, we think God didn't answer our prayers. It is sometimes in God's unanswered prayers that we later discover his answer was the perfect plan.

What If God Doesn't Answer Your Prayer?

This is taken from a song by Garth Brooks that talks about Unanswered Prayers...

"Sometimes I thank God, for unanswered prayers. Remember when you're talking to the Man upstairs, just because he don't answer, doesn't mean He don't care...Some of God's greatest gifts, are unanswered prayers."

So often we make the mistake of thinking that if we say our prayers and we don't get what we asked for, the Lord has deserted us; that He didn't answer our prayers. Just as the sentiment in the song suggests, some of God's greatest gifts are those things that we never would have prayed for.

This is not in any way to suggests that when a child gets sick, it is a gift. The gift was the child in the first place. We don't know why some things happen, but it is only in knowing there is no answer to some questions that we will be able to achieve peace.

Prayers Answered

A little girl had been given three months to live by her doctors. Her family enlisted the prayers of everyone they knew. "Please pray for our little girl," they said. Every day the little girl got weaker and weaker and grew sicker and sicker. Still they prayed, "Dear God please make our daughter well. Take away her pain, let her run and play like the other children."

One day the brave child smiled her last smile, and squeezed her mother's hand for the last time. As she took her last breath, they noticed how peaceful she looked. She was no longer tensed up with the pain that had imprisoned her. Her steroid swollen face even looked 'normal' again.

As they looked at the lifeless body of their beloved little girl, her parents suddenly realized: God had indeed answered their prayers. She was well; she was in Heaven, running and playing with the other angels.

Show Me A Sign

There is a popular saying these days that "If God Had A Refrigerator, Your Picture Would Be On It." The pictures we hang on our refrigerators are either drawn by someone very special to us, or they are taken of our loved ones and friends. We only hang up special people's pictures on our ice box. You are that special person to the Lord. He loves you. He takes great delight in knowing you and watching you. He rejoices when you rejoice, and he cries when you cry. The Lord is always there for you.

These days we get so many negative messages every day. The news is bad, people's language is getting worse. We are bombarded with commercials, and constant reminders of things we would like to forget. Why not try this?

Why not put prayerful thoughts and positive messages on pieces of paper and hang them in your house. I have a sign that says "Count Your Blessings" on top of my television. Every time we watch tv we see that little message. You could hang a sign on your refrigerator that says "God Loves You" or "Thank You God For Our Blessings," or "As For Me and My House, We Will Serve The Lord.."

The more positive messages you have around your house, the more times you and your family will be reminded of what is good in this world. The love of Jesus Christ is very good.

The 23rd Psalm--It is a prayer that will give you peace.

The Lord is my shepherd, I shall not want. He makes me lie down in green pastures; He leads me beside still waters; He restores my soul. He leads me in the right paths for his name's sake.
Even though I walk through the darkest valley, I fear no evil; for You are with me; your rod and your staff--they comfort me. You prepare a table before me in the presence of my enemies; You anoint my head with oil; my cup overflows. Surely goodness and mercy shall follow me all the days of my life, and I shall dwell in the house of the LORD my whole life long.

Dear Lord,
As I sit here alone, I am in wonder at all you have done for me. The things I've done, the things I've seen, o Lord thank you for all of the opportunities you have given me. Even through my losses or setbacks, you have provided me with your peace and when I've looked for it, you've opened windows I could never have imagined. Thank you for continuing to be with me and give me peace. Amen .

During Periods Of Rain In Your Life...Pray Through It

When all you can do is pray...then do just that. Pray like you mean it, pray like there's no tomorrow, pray like your life depends on it, and then wake up tomorrow and pray again.

The Lord is there for you. People are there for you. You just have to do your part and be there for yourself. Be kind to yourself, at least as kind as you are to others.

Don't ever give up on any situation, no matter how bleak it may seem or how scary it may seem. Most things look a whole lot better in the morning. You will get past this, and someday you will look back on this time.

There will be lessons learned, relationships formed and strengthened, and faith renewed. Hopefully, you will be there to help someone else who is going through a tough time some day in the future.

Stay in God's world and He will stay in yours. May God bless you in your time of need and may this book provide you with some peaceful and positive thoughts.

You Can Find Peace In The Rain

Rain often gets a bad rap. Picnics and ballgames are cancelled due to rain. When rain gets out of control it can cause damage, tornadoes, and other weather related disasters. Just one look up at a rain threatening, dark, clouded sky can send chills of fear through some people.

Because I married a man named Rains, I notice this negative connotation maybe more than most people. I also notice the good the rain does.

There would be no spring flowers if there were no rains. There would be no lakes and rivers, and no wonderful, lazy, rainy days to force us to stay inside and rest.

Rain makes the world more beautiful and it makes the plants stronger. This is how it is in our lives. We can make it through the rains and come out a stronger and more beautiful person.

Just as a bud develops into many petals which make up a lovely flower, we can emerge from the storms of our lives with new facets that we never imagined. As long as we look towards the sunshine we can become stronger than we ever thought we could.

Notes (Favorite Bible verses, motivational sayings)

_____

_____

_____

_____

_____

_____

_____

_____

_____

_____

_____

_____

_____

Bibliography:

Prayer is Good Medicine by Larry Dossey, M.D.; Harper Collins, New York, New York 1996

Talking With God, A Guide To Prayer by Mack B. Stokes; Abingdon Press, Nashville, TN 1989

Apples of Gold, Compiled by Jo Petty; Published by C.R. Gibson Company, Norwalk, Connecticut, Copyright MCMLXII

America's God and Country- Encyclopedia of Quotations by William J. Federer; Fame Publishing Inc., 1996

Playing on His Team by Sally and Rob Rains; Crosstraining Publishing Co., NE 1997

Positive People Newsletter; by Jim Gentile, internet, Nov. 2002

Believing In Ourselves: The Wisdom of Women; Ariel Books, Andrews and McMeel, Kansas City, MO 64112

Why Do Good People Suffer? Growing Christians Bible Life Church, United Methodist Church Resource; Graded Press, 1987

Simple Abundance, A Daybook of Comfort and Joy; Sarah Ban Breathnach; Warner Books, 1995

Illuminated Prayers by Marianne Williamson

Keeping Your Kids Grounded When You're Flying By The Seat Of Your Pants by Dr. Tim Jordan and Sally Tippett Rains; Palmerston and Reed Publishing Co. 2000.

The Purpose Driven Life by Rick Warren; Zondervan; Grand Rapids Michigan 2002

It's Your Turn Now by Debra D. Peppers, Ph.D.; Impact Christian Books, St. Louis, MO 2001

RaiNBoWS FoR KiDs
Giving Kids Something To Look Forward To
a 501 (c) (3) charity

If you would like to help others find peace in the rain, please consider supporting Rainbows For Kids which helps children with cancer and other serious diseases or conditions and their families.

The family of a young cancer patient found out how useful a positive attitude is in getting through a difficult situation, so with the help of family, friends, and total strangers, Rainbows For Kids was started.

Rainbows For Kids helps in three areas:
1) Provide fun activities and support for the families in the Greater St. Louis area
2) Support national cancer and illness related causes (including research searching for a cure)
3) Pray for the families-- Rainbow Prayer Chain

Please remember Rainbows when you need to send a gift, make a tribute or just want to contribute to a charity.

Rainbows For Kids
P.O. Box 260027
St. Louis, MO 63126

www.rainbowsforkids.org

About The Author

Sally Tippett Rains is the author of nine books including two Christian books, three coaching books (written with sports coaches), and her most recent, *Get Going Girl! Lessons learned from a Fourth Grader.* Rains is also a songwriter and speaker with Go Girl Luncheons, which are monthly motivational lunches for women in St. Louis. She lives with her husband Rob and their two sons B.J. and Mike in St. Louis, MO.

The author welcomes e-mails from readers. Send e-mails to: info@AllStarIdeas.com

To order additional copies of this book, please send $20 plus $5 for shipping and handling to:

All Star Ideas
P.O. Box 270518
St. Louis, MO 63127

www.AllStarIdeas.com

Other Books By Sally Tippett Rains

Get Going Girl, Lessons Learned From a Fourth Grader
2005, Power Publishing, St. Louis, MO

Baseball A to Z, produced by St. Louis Pinch-Hitters in conjunction with the Cardinals Wives and Cardinals Care. 2003, St. Louis, MO

The Mighty MOX, (with Rob Rains) 2001 Diamond Communications, Southbend, IN

The Pope's Visit To the USA (with David Klocek), 2000, Palmerston and Reed Publishers

Keeping Your Kids Grounded When Your're Flying By The Seat Of Your Pants, 2000, Palmerston and Reed Publishers, St. Lous, MO

Playing On His Team (with Rob Rains),1999, Crosstraining Publishing, Omaha, NE

The following sports books published by Coaches Choice Books, Monterey, CA 1998
  Drills and Skills for Basketball, (with Rich Grawer)
  How to Play and Coach Baseball (with Wendall Kim)
  Softball Pitching Fundamentals (w/ Carie Dever-Boaz)

Printed in the United States
35396LVS00002BA/187-411